THE WAY OF THE ROAD WARRIOR

THE WAY OF THE ROAD WARRIOR

Lessons in Business and Life from the Road Most Traveled

ROBERT L. JOLLES

Foreword by
F. W. Sanzenbacher

JOSSEY-BASS
A Wiley Imprint
www.josseybass.com

Published by Jossey-Bass
A Wiley Imprint
989 Market Street, San Francisco, CA 94103-1741   www.josseybass.com

Jossey-Bass books and products are available through most bookstores.
To contact Jossey-Bass directly call our Customer Care Department within the U.S. at
800-956-7739, outside the U.S. at 317-572-3986, or fax 317-572-4002.

Jossey-Bass also publishes its books in a variety of electronic formats. Some content that
appears in print may not be available in electronic books.

Library of Congress Cataloging-in-Publication Data

Jolles, Robert L., 1957-
 The way of the road warrior : lessons in business and life from the road most
traveled / by Robert L. Jolles ; foreword by F.W. Sanzenbacher.—1st ed.
   p. cm.
 ISBN-13: 978-0-7879-8062-7 (alk. paper)
 ISBN-10: 0-7879-8062-5 (alk. paper)
 1. Business travel. I. Title.
 G156.5.B86J65 2006 910'.2—dc22   2005023417

Printed in the United States of America
FIRST EDITION
HB Printing   10 9 8 7 6 5 4 3 2

CONTENTS

This book is dedicated to my Road Warrior brothers and sisters. You are a hearty lot, but you are not impervious to the pain and loneliness that life on the road can bring. It is my hope that within these pages, you find humor, comfort, empathy, and inspiration that contribute to your survival on the road—as well as to the survival of those you love who are waiting at home.

FOREWORD
"THE SOBs IN THE METAL TUBE"

It is ironic that someone who has influenced my life so greatly should be a total stranger, someone whose name I can't even remember properly. I once even went to the library to search in the encyclopedia, but could find no reference. Perhaps I had remembered the spelling incorrectly. After all, I am a pilot and deal mostly with numbers.

But yet I had been so impressed by something this person wrote that I penned the words into a personal journal, and through a war in Southeast Asia, the joys and challenges of personal relationships, and the myriad ups and downs of growing older, I have reverted to its guidance. It has always proven to be a true companion. Words of wisdom that today's air traveler should always keep in mind—or anyone, for that matter.

You see, the author did not just dwell on his main topic, military matters, strategy, and tactics—or, I should say as a pilot—on weather, mechanical problems, and traffic delays. He told the story through the faces and feelings of people. What he showed was that it is the battle fought within ourselves that is often the most difficult. The frustration and anger caused by the lack of

---

After this Foreword was submitted for publication, I finally learned the source of the quote at the end: *Battle Studies: Ancient and Modern Battle*, by Colonel Charles-Jean-Jacques-Joseph Ardant du Picq, a nineteenth-century French military historian. His words have stood the test of time indeed.

caring and selfishness of people who should have cared cause the deepest hurt: An internal scar that we will carry home with us.

And so it seems to an airline passenger when caught in an extensive delay and told nothing about what is going on. People who should care about you and your problems just don't. And as anyone who has experienced "a bad travel day" in our nation's skies knows, it can truly test the human spirit.

After thirty years as an airline pilot, I have encountered a few of these "bad travel days" and find it amazing that lack of communication between the cockpit and cabin even happens. After all, the pilots and passengers are all in the same boat . . . or should I say airplane?

Most pilots empathize with the plight of the passenger; after all, more than half the pilots I have worked with commuted to their base from a distant city as airline passengers. "Been there, done that, got the T-shirt." I feel the same infuriating helplessness and frustration that the passenger does. Perhaps the key word here is *feel*. That must be there. If the pilot does not care, the war of communications is lost.

Most pilots are well aware of how important schedule dependability is to the passenger. It is part of the three S's: safety, schedule, and service. Merely scanning the boarding area or walking through the cabin can show you—every flight has a hundred or more stories to be viewed, and each one is important to its main character.

Now, let's think about the ones Rob Jolles calls "Road Warriors" for a minute. To me, they are the bread and butter of the airline industry. They are also the most dependent upon it. You see, for the Road Warriors, getting to their destination on time will determine a sale made, an appointment met, a lecture presented, or a conference attended. Based on those things, at stake can be a promotion received, paycheck earned, or a project won. It can eventually come down to a family cared for or even a college tuition covered. You see, I don't really see them as Road Warriors, or even passengers. They are *people*. People with a great deal at stake.

In the jargon of a captain, I am required to know how many "SOBs" are in the cabin. One morning I asked the chief flight attendant this question as we started a flight and was told very firmly that I shouldn't refer to our passengers that way. He was new—just out of training, and didn't know any better. He didn't know that "S-O-B" meant *soul on board*. That ultimately is what every passenger is: a soul, a spirit. You have to care about people because it affects the human spirit. Even yours, for sometimes it helps us all keep going.

But it can work positively also. For instance, there's nothing like the smiles of relaxed couples returning from holiday. Or the suntanned faces and the packages and souvenirs that follow them on board.

The Road Warriors have different signs that are equally obvious. In place of the souvenirs are the cell phones, laptop computers, and attaché cases spilled onto the tray table. For some, it may be an unbuttoned collar and loosened tie, the slight upturn around the corner of the mouth, or the eyes closed in rest: all signs of a good case of "I'm-going-home-itis," and very nice to see.

Routine announcements are a universal way of saying "you are important." It can be as simple as "the weather is still good in San Francisco and we will be landing on schedule." Not everyone is plugged into the National Weather Service or has an airspeed indicator in front of them.

Sometimes it can be as simple as remembering to say, "On the left side of the aircraft is the Grand Canyon." Although the pilot may fly over it twenty times in a month, it may be a once-in-a-lifetime occurrence for some of the passengers aboard. I just don't understand why this experience can't be shared. It takes so little effort.

For some people, the content of the announcement is not the most important part. It is the sound of a confident, honest voice that may ease the anxiety of a first flight in an airplane. After a period of turbulence during thunderstorm season, even the most seasoned Road Warrior likes to hear, "We are now in clear skies."

After all, it is rather unnatural to be sealed in a metal tube, shot through the air at six hundred miles per hour, and have no control over the outcome. It requires trust, and that trust deserves consideration. The two can only be bound with true spirit. True spirit that looks outward to recognize others and act for their benefit whenever possible—even if only to say, "I don't know."

I have never been a "machine" man. How I ended up spending so much of my life inside one is a puzzle. More than twenty-five thousand hours sealed inside a machine. That's three years of my life not even having set foot on this earth. Perhaps this is why my wife jokingly says I am so out of it! But I don't think I could have done it without other people having been there. People in the cockpit and people in the cabin. People! Because it is people that have spirit. There is no spirit in a machine without people.

Oh yes, the quotation! I almost forgot . . .

"It is the spirit which wins battles and will always win them, just as it has won them in all periods of the world's history. The spiritual and moral qualities of war have not changed since those days. Mechanical devices, precision weapons, all the thunderbolts invented by man and his sciences will never get the better of that thing—called the human spirit."

A lifetime of lessons that affect the human spirit can be learned from the road. Enjoy your journey . . .

August 2005   F. W. Sanzenbacher
Retired Captain, United Airlines

Wednesday, October 8th–9:00 P.M.
The work I have scheduled for tomorrow is work I have performed hundreds of times. I've just finished my room service meal, the ball game on ESPN is a blowout, and it's time to break out the laptop to reflect on a business thought that was running through my mind today . . .

I am a "Road Warrior." I have spent nearly twenty years of my life conducting business on the road. I am a corporate trainer, but that is irrelevant for these pages. My real occupation is to survive and thrive on the road.

I am not alone—not by a long shot. Millions of Americans share my journeys on the road. They are sales reps, managers, doctors, lawyers, engineers, scientists, military personnel, entrepreneurs, computer professionals, butchers, bakers, and candlestick makers. I've sat next to and listened to them all—even the candlestick makers.

I am writing for *these* people. This is not to say that many others, including casual travelers, may not learn the lessons that appear in these pages, as well. Please, be my guest. These lessons are not reserved for the Road Warrior alone. I just want to warn you. Some of the lessons and travel tips might seem a bit farfetched, but anyone who takes the office on the road will not see it that way.

I do not claim to be a Road Warrior genius, but I am what I call "methodically observant." Let me tell you what I mean by that last statement. A number of years ago, after I completed my first book, I had what I called at the time "a writing void." I had been used to writing, almost conditioned to write. I took pride in authoring my books in airports, on planes, in cabs and hotel rooms, but never at home. Being on the road brutalized my family enough without my adding to it by sneaking off to write. Nope, my writing took place on the road.

Besides, what was I to write about? My book was at the publishers, moving through the halls from one editor to the next. I couldn't seriously begin a new writing project. I hadn't finished the first one yet! I was on call, making simple editing changes, carrying a laptop but no longer seriously using it for writing. I was on hold, with no more stories waiting to be written.

This didn't mean I didn't have stories to tell. After each trip, I would come home and have stories—lots of them. Some of the stories were happy, and some were sad. Some conveyed the loneliness of a Road Warrior's frequent solitary confinement, and some were about the people I met and the joys of my adventures.

My wife could see it when I walked into the house. She could see it on my face and hear it in my voice. A hundred thousand miles a year on the road will have that effect on you. There has always been one critical rule for my storytelling. I must have my audience's undivided attention. As a professional speaker, you might call it professional courtesy, but I am hurt and offended when I can't hold the attention of my own family. I speak in front of thousands of people a year, but my toughest audience has always been my family.

My wife knows this finicky little quirk of mine so we've developed a system. If it's a story for the kids, I tell the kids before bedtime. If it isn't, we put the kids to bed, clear the decks of all critical news, and away I go.

If we have company, I will ask permission from our guests to have my storytelling time. If they don't agree to the rules (to keep quiet and listen), I will tell my story another time.

It was during one of these "guest sessions" that it happened. I wrapped up what I thought was a damn good story when one of my wife's friends asked me if I ever wrote these stories down.

I felt like I was watching one of the old Reese's Cup commercials where two people collide. One is carrying chocolate and the other is carrying peanut butter. As they get up, one says to the other, "Hey, you got peanut butter on my chocolate!" The other says, "Yeah, well, you got chocolate on my peanut butter!" The rest was history.

A great idea was hatched. I had a writing void that needed to be filled, and I now had material. Both had been there the whole time. From that day forward, I have kept a journal of all my travels. It is now well over a thousand pages long! When I began it, I figured I would be able to capture some of the adventures I was living as a Road Warrior. I had no idea that the biggest benefit of all was yet to be discovered from this simple little exercise in writing.

You see, my journal has taught me about my business—and my life. It has gone far beyond a collection of stories. It has become my bible of learning. I may have *thought* I was putting these words together to collect my memories, but it just didn't work out that way.

When I began my entries, I would comment on what was before me, what I could see and remember. However, the more I wrote about these events, the more I questioned what was before me, what I saw and how I remembered it. It helped me discover and learn from what I was living and not to simply comment on it. Later in this book, I will suggest, beg, and implore you to keep a journal. For now, however, let me tell you a little more about mine.

By capturing these events through the years, I can now play back for you critical discoveries. The effort has allowed me to talk to you about surviving the rigors of the road, and I can share some valuable life lessons learned. Many of these lessons are right there in front of everyone; we just don't see them clearly. I would like to be your spectacles and put these lessons in focus.

To help us keep our sanity intact, we Road Warriors build walls to keep our home lives separate from our lives on the road. I want to jump up on that wall and peer over it.

I want to celebrate these lessons, which I hope will take on many different forms. At times, I am sure they will be new to you. At times they will act as gentle reminders of ideas you have learned from the past. They are lessons just the same, and I look forward to you, my reader, examining them with me.

In case you were wondering, this isn't your typical business book. It is certainly nothing like my two earlier books. I do not pretend here to give you the twenty-three secrets of success, and I can't even tell you how to find lost luggage at baggage claim (except to advise you *never* to use baggage claim unless unavoidable; more on this later). You'll find that I'm less interested in telling you what to do than in sharing bits and pieces of my firsthand experience.

I've tried to organize these around the lessons they taught me, but you might find different lessons in them—that's your right. So this book is more in the nature of a series of meditations than a book on business hardball. I hope you'll bear with me.

Saying this, my editor asked me to say a few words here about the theme of this book, and it's not difficult to express this as I take a step back and reflect on a life on the road. People come first. It doesn't matter that most of the people the Road Warrior meets are strangers; from cabbies to A.V. technicians, from CEOs to family members, they are all on the Road Warrior's team. If you ever face the hard choice between the road and the people who matter most to you, I hope this book will have helped prepare you for that, too.

In the chapters that follow, you'll find a series of lessons applicable to business and life that I discovered on the road, during those long trips across the country, lengthy taxi rides, and endless nights in hotel rooms. They're enlivened by excerpts from my journals of the day, presented with the most minimal of edits. I'm one who believes you can't go back and edit feelings and emotions you are trying to articulate from a specific moment in time; in fact, it's these experiences and emotions that are the backbone of the lessons you are about to wander through.

OK, here we go. Get ready to pick up a travel tip here and there and enjoy. I'll be glad to show you how to survive, thrive, and outsmart just about any aspect of travel you may endure. But be forewarned and be wary, my friends. I have faith that you will find far more than travel tips. I hope these pages offer many lessons that will not only enrich your life but help you to make the most of your life as well. Sit back, buckle up, leave your Road Warrior suitcase in the closet, and take a ride with me. While on this journey,

I want you to remember one simple quote that came to me years ago on a redeye from Los Angeles to Washington. At 3:00 A.M., in an uncomfortable Road Warrior stupor between sleep and waking, my mind was wrestling with a true definition for the word *wisdom*. Out came the following words . . .

> *Wisdom consists of three things:*
> *Success, failure, and a conscious knowledge of the lessons*
> *learned from each.*

When you've completed your journey to end of this book, I think this definition will make a lot more sense.

Great Falls, Virginia   Robert L. Jolles
August 2005

CHAPTER ONE

Some Days Are Better Than Others

When I went to the University of Maryland, I began as a business major. I studied mostly general business, accounting, and economics. After I graduated, I went to work for the New York Life Insurance Company and felt my lessons in business and life were complete. I had no idea how naive I was. No, in fact, the greatest lessons I would ever learn in business were yet to come in the years ahead on the road. Put in two million miles in the air and you'll learn a lot more than how to get your luggage stowed on board an airplane.

"Some days are better than others" quite simply implies that we start with a careful look at the reality of living—day, by day, by day. In business, I believe you're as good as your last interaction with your customer. (As my kids get older, I'm beginning to believe that a father is only as good as his last interaction as well.) That's not intended to be a cynical comment but rather a realistic warning. I suppose one of the keys to being a success, in business or in life, is to simply prove on a consistent basis that you are who you say you are. When you're not feeling in great physical or emotional shape, however, you still have to play your best—your customers expect no less. This first chapter is about facing this perennial Road Warrior challenge.

In your way stand a number of telling obstacles. What happens when you are not at the top of your game? How will you cope with sickness or physical pain when you have no choice but to do your job? When you are faced with cultural differences, how will you respond? What happens when grief and depression disrupt your life, and how will you gain perspective to battle these obstacles? At the risk of starting this book on a downbeat, I'd like to share some of the tougher days—if you can weather the storm through days like these, the victories that follow will be even sweeter.

Giving It Your Best

A fact of life in business is, quite simply, you can't always be at your best. Road Warriors know this because so many factors can affect their performances. A missed flight, a bad cabbie, a difficult client—the list can go on and on. The fact of the matter is, how will you perform when you don't want to perform?

Thursday, June 6th–4:55 P.M.

I certainly saw it coming. My travels have taken me to Madison, Wisconsin. This was not one of my best two-day classes. As a matter of fact, I would rate it as one of my worst. I came into town tired. I woke up tired. I spent eight hours trying to manufacture energy and grew more tired. I went out with the customer and was tired. I went to bed and woke up tired and spent the rest of the day tired. I feel old. Like a jockey on a racehorse, I went for the crop, beat on the horse, and the horse just didn't respond.

Oh, I've got my excuses, but unfortunately, they are just that; excuses. Back-to-back two-day classes. A small audience in a large room. Oh, and one last thing. Although I spent a lot of time leaning on the walls, I did not sit. I may not have been as good as I wanted to be, but I did not quit. I gave it my all. I tried as hard as

I could. In this case, that may not have been good enough, but I
sure did try. This is what I take with me from this week. As tired,
burned out, and beat as I was, I didn't mail it in.

Nobody I know purposely takes on a job with the intent of not doing the best they can. Unfortunately, outside distractions can seriously impact what it is you are trying to accomplish. If your job requires energy and thought the next day, you learn early, even if you have to wear sunglasses to make sure you get to your room without being distracted, you get to that room and rest up. Of course, just because you are in your room, there is no guarantee that you'll get a good night's sleep . . .

Early to bed and early to rise can sometimes take a back seat to reality in the world of the Road Warrior. You see, there is an exception to the rule, and the rule is called, "All rules are off when it comes to redeye flights." I would like to kick things off with a whopper of a story. This story has no great redeeming value, nor does it contribute mightily to the lessons I wish to share with you. If nothing else, however, I hope it will prove that I've earned my stripes, and it might even get me the sympathy vote with the tougher book reviewers.

As our story unfolds, we find our hero, Road Warrior Rob, getting set for a three-day traveling blitz that starts in Cleveland. I call this story, "The Mother of All Redeyes."

Tuesday, April 28th–2:25 P.M.
This week could be called, "The Week to Catch Up on Air Miles"
week. I'm not earning a whole lot, but I'm going to be flying a
whole lot.

Today, I head to Cleveland. I'll be checking into the Renaissance Hotel and resting up for tomorrow. I have an all-day session that begins at 8:00 A.M. for Nat City. This is the last of five that I will be doing—although they just merged, so there should be more down the road.

My biggest challenge for tomorrow is to get this class finished by 3:00 P.M. My flight is at 3:50 to San Francisco. Miss it, and it will make this trip a lot more complicated than I would like. Cleveland, here I come.

Wednesday, April 29th—4:30 P.M.

Good-bye, Cleveland. After a mad dash from my training session, I am airborne and on my way west—way west. First, of course, I needed to make it interesting. Class finished at 3:15, leaving me 15–20 minutes to drive to the airport and catch a 3:50 flight. I'm really trying to cut down on these mad rushes to the airport, but it was either catch this flight or spend the night in Cleveland.

Now, this day is going to last a good, long time. I'm on my way to San Francisco, landing around 6:10 P.M. their time. I have to change airlines—which means a long walk—and catch a 7:00 P.M. to Honolulu. It is what the airlines call an illegal connection, because it doesn't provide the 55 minutes required for connections. I'll take my chances or sleep in San Francisco tonight. Either way, I'm OK, because I don't speak until tomorrow night. Right now, the travel gods are looking kindly on me. We are due in early to San Francisco.

Wednesdayish, April 29th—5:10 P.M.

Well, that's what time I'm pretending it is. Actually, it's 12:10 A.M., but I've switched to Hawaii time. All systems are go and touchdown

*in Honolulu is set for 9:30 P.M. (3:30 A.M. East Coast time). I'm fight-
ing off sleep right now. I want to make sure I can sleep when I
finally arrive. I also want to be fresh when I speak tomorrow night
. . . at 5:30 P.M. Hawaii time–11:30 P.M. East Coast time.*

Wednesdayish, April 29th–10:00 P.M.

*My cab driver has stopped to fill up his gas tank. I've been up now
for about 22 hours. We're still about 25 minutes from the hotel. I
know I'll get to sleep pretty quickly when I hit the pillow. I'm just
wondering how long I'll stay down. I'm figuring that by the time I
get to sleep, it will be about 5:00 A.M., my time.*

Thursday, April 30th–6:15 A.M.

*Good news. I slept pretty damn well. I'm rested and ready to roll.
Now I've got stay busy until it's my time . . . like 11 more hours. I'm
sitting out on my balcony watching the sun come up over the
Pacific Ocean. I guess there are worse places to have to kill time.*

Thursdayish, April 30th–9:45 P.M.

*I'm airborne and beginning my journey home. The presentation
was a struggle, but it's behind me now. I blew a fuse in my power
strip, sweat all over the equipment, but gutted out a pretty good
talk. I'm on a redeye heading back to Los Angeles. We were due in
at 5:15 A.M. Now we've been told we'll be in around 4:45 A.M. I'm not
sure if that's good news or not. My flight for Washington doesn't
leave until 8:00 A.M.*

Fridayish, May 1st–4:50 A.M.

*I guess that's what time it is. I've decided that I'm somewhere in
time limbo. If I go with Hawaiian time, which I just left, it's 1:50 A.M.*

If I go with California time, which I'm on right now, it's 4:50 A.M. However, in about three and a half hours I should be taking off and heading home. That would make it 7:50 A.M. That's the one I like best! Yes, I'm making it 7:50 A.M. Oh my God, I think I'm delirious!

I think I slept on the plane for about an hour. That's what I'm telling myself, at least. Now, I have found a pretty nice-looking bench to sleep on while I wait for my next flight. It doesn't take off until 8:05 A.M. (uh, this time). I've got what appears to be a couple of strange-looking people sleeping pretty close by. I must have found a good place for street people to want to sleep here. I've made a pillow out of my suitcases with my LCD projector carrying case strap under my head. I've even set my travel alarm. Hopefully, I can find one or two more hours. Good night, limbo.

Friday, May 1st—8:35 A.M.

Finally, I'm actually heading home on my last flight. I got one more hour of sleep with my unsavory friends. I'm pretty sure that right about now, you couldn't tell us apart. I'm look awfully beaten up. My butt hurts already, and I've got four more hours to go. I feel pretty rested, though, and my competitive side has actually enjoyed this little battle with sleep. Somewhere along these last two flights, it became Friday. At least the week is over. I can honestly say these have been the longest three days I think I have ever spent in my life.

Of course it's a little unusual to go from the Midwest to Hawaii and back to the East Coast, all for one hour's worth of work, but it happens in the world of the Road Warrior. If nothing else, it certainly has made me less fearful of a little old California-to-D.C.

redeye. Pshaw, that's nothing! It's just another fact of life when giving it your best.

Coping with Sickness

You can't always wait for perfect health—physical or mental—before hitting the road. With planes to catch, appointments to make, or in my case, seminars to conduct, sometimes you just have to suck it up.

> ### Monday, December 13th—6:15 A.M.
>
> *Here's a switch. I'm an hour early for my return flight, I've got a confirmed aisle seat, the plane is in, we seem to be proceeding without delays, and I'm terrified. I've been fighting off a cold for a couple of days, and sometime last night, it finally struck. I've already taken a Claritin, and it's no use. My sinuses are a mess, my nose is leaking like a sieve, and I'm in trouble.*
>
> *Once we get airborne, I'm expecting excruciating pain, and there's not a damn thing I can do about it but take it like a man. Each flight I've taken on this trip over the last three days has been more painful than the last, but this has the makings of being the Mother of All Earache plane trips.*
>
> *I feel like an inmate on death row. My decongestant will not commute my sentence. Soon the warden will load me into my torture chamber, and I will be in agony for the next hour and change . . . if I'm lucky.*

When I went to school, I used to pride myself on my perfect attendance. There were textbooks I skimmed, lectures I slept through, and study sessions—well let's just say I could have taken them a little more seriously. Classes, however, I never missed. Sickness was out of the question.

If I woke up in the morning not feeling well, my mother would smile and assure me I wasn't sick. She would tell me I merely had morning sickness, and it would pass. I'm embarrassed to say, it wasn't until I was in my late twenties and married that I had the term *morning sickness* properly defined for me.

Adhering to the Laws of the Land

While we're on the topic of giving it your best, keep an eye out for roadblocks that might stand in your way. In business, certain rules and laws need to be followed. One is to listen and respect the information that is presented to you—if someone has warned you about the food, the water, the weather, whatever, heed the warning. Eating on the road can be an adventure of the worst kind. That's why, after the novelty and thrill of road travel wears off, most Road Warriors prefer to kick back, order room service, and watch some tube. Besides, it's safer eating in the hotel . . . isn't it? (Warning: if you feel you may have a weak constitution, you might want to skip ahead a few pages.)

Friday, March 5th–5:25 P.M.
Ah, lovely Cancun, Mexico. Despite being over the border, everything seems American. A few months ago, I was invited to give a presentation here, and since I had never been to Cancun, I was excited.

When I got to my room last night, I was tired and hungry. I have had three seminars in three days in three cities, and none of the trips were easy. I looked through the room service menu and prepared to order. I was told everything, including the water, was safe here, but I was skeptical. With a seminar first thing in the morning, I just couldn't drink the water, but I did decide to go with some rather exotic dishes.

I feel asleep around midnight and had a dream that I was being pursued by a skunk. I tried to run but I couldn't get away from the horrendous smell. I was running, and running, and running.

At four in the morning I woke up. Let's just say that what I had been running from was not entirely a dream. It was either me that was creating the hideous smell I was dreaming of, or a skunk truly did jump into my room, make itself comfortable, and leave. I was in the bathroom until five.

At six in the morning I woke up again. I didn't have the same dream, but the results were the same. Every fifteen minutes, I ran to the bathroom. I still think I resembled Charles Shultz's loveable character Pigpen. Instead of a cloud of dirt following me everywhere, there was simply a cloud of odor.

I venture to guess that you, too, have been in this condition once or twice in your life. But I'll bet you didn't have to get up and speak in front of 250 financial consultants for a one-hour, high-energy talk!

At 7:00 A.M., my cloud and I left the hotel room and floated downstairs. I wasn't nauseous, but my stomach was a mess. Now I began to appeal to two of our human senses as I worked to set up the room. I was not only appealing to the sense of smell. For the first time in my life, I honestly could not control the, uh, sounds I was making. These weren't little toots, either. I simply had no control of what was trying work its way through my system.

Finally, 8:00 A.M. rolled around and so did I. Miraculously, although I was uncomfortable, I held up well. I did toot a couple of times, but I think I got away with it. The first time it happened, I cleared my throat imitating the sound and moved on. The second time it happened, I wasn't as lucky. It was loud, and all I could do was pound on one of my books that was nearby. I don't think anyone thought I was tooting, but I could see confusion in the audience's eyes. I could sense they were collectively asking, "Why did that guy just lose control of himself and smack his own book for no apparent reason?" It was a quick decision, but I figured a small spastic attack was better than the alternative.

I think that simply looking like a buffoon was the right choice, but it's not the main point of that Road Warrior confession. Watch what you put in your mouth. Just because it is hotel food, that doesn't mean it's safe. If you are out of the country, my advice is, *don't* take their word for it. Don't drink the water, and watch those exotic dishes.

Coping With Pain

Although some of the younger readers might think physical breakdowns aren't in store for them, the fact is that business travel is physically demanding and takes a toll—but that doesn't mean our clients feel sorry for us.

Tuesday, July 7th–7:00 A.M.

From the medical desk, I had some minor surgery earlier this week and I have about 40 stitches in my back. It hurts like hell, but I've got a job to do. The client who hired me three months ago doesn't want to hear about my troubles. I was careful bringing in the equipment, and as long as I don't flail too much, everything should hold together. I do want to be careful, though.

Road Warriors are a tough lot, and in business, that's not such a bad trait to develop. Athletes play in pain. In business, sometimes, Road Warriors have to do the same.

Everyone has an Achilles heel of sorts. For me, it's my neck. After years of marathon running and triathlons, the miles caught up with me. I bid farewell to my love of running and replaced it with swimming, but my neck provides me with an occasional unwelcome souvenir.

7:30 P.M.

Ouch. My neck is killing me. I certainly could have done without a five-hour flight while trying to nurse this thing back to health. I'm praying it lets up a little bit more tomorrow, because I'm awfully tight.

All appears well, except for my neck. I'm in agony. As one who always looks to the brighter side, in a way, I'm fortunate. Although the pain is excruciating, my neck is not locked, as it commonly is when I have an episode like this. This simply means my condition is not obvious to others. No one will know but me.

I remember a saying about runners that I felt at the time. Only a runner would understand:

"Runners are the sickest group of healthy people you will ever meet."

Stop and think about that quote for a minute. I will add another class of individuals who should understand just as well.

With the lifting, running, sweating, and hustling, I believe the Road Warriors qualify for that quote, as well. We are some of the sickest healthy people you will ever meet.

Depression

Not all pain is physical. No matter who you are, life as a Road Warrior brings you face-to-face with depression. You can't leave the family, accept the pressure, catch the cab and airplane, check into the hotel, and do the job you are traveling to complete without some down days.

Friday, September 26th—1:00 P.M.

I'm airborne and heading home. I think I'd just as soon forget this week. The irony is that it follows such a good week. If I walked on the moon last week, I walked in mud this week. This trip started with a tearful good-bye from my youngest. That was like a shot to the stomach. The cab was late, the plane was delayed, and a nasty stewardess continued my spiral. Then there was the seminar.

Today's seminar just didn't seem to have the spark I normally like. Usually, I think it out, troubleshoot the problem and generate solutions to fix it. I don't really have a clue why this seminar didn't go better.

Time? Maybe. Perhaps they were hungry, but I was the first speaker they saw. Maybe it was the seating. Maybe it was just a somewhat burned-out Rob. The last couple of weeks have been intense. I was up at 4:30 A.M. this morning. I just haven't had a normal sleep pattern with a normal morning in weeks. The other day I looked back over the calendar. I haven't slept in (sleeping past 8:15 A.M.), in almost four months.

*Maybe I'm going to go through some sort of a letdown, I don't
know, but I know I'm going through something this week.*

When we are sick, one of the most disconcerting problems
often lies in not knowing what is making us sick. It's almost a relief
when a doctor comes in with a definitive answer of some sort.

Road Warriors must cope with depression that often supplies
no definitive answers. Yes, the canceled flight or the nasty flight
companion can exacerbate it, but sometimes it's a little harder to
identify the source.

As a person whose professional study has been mainly related
to selling, I know the biggest objection people typically have is,
quite simply, a fear of the unknown. Now, I'm no psychologist, but
if you are going to try and get through a Road Warrior's depression, it might be a good idea to try and figure out what exactly has
you down.

Friday, September 22nd–2:00 A.M.

*It's 2:00 A.M. and I'm getting banged around in the back of a cab
somewhere near San Diego. Our flight was late, and we now have a
long drive up the coast. I've been on the road the entire week, and
I feel as if I have gone twelve rounds in a boxing match. Five seminars in four cities will do that to you.*

*The real battle here, however, is not physical, it's mental. I can
get through the lack of sleep and the hours on my feet. The question is, can I get through the emotional battle that seems to be
scarring my soul?*

*I have been playing my picture frame and looking at some
scanned pictures on my laptop. It's helping.*

The "playing my picture frame" reference comes from a little gift I bought myself from the Sharper Image catalog a couple of years ago. My picture frame, which is small and portable, not only holds a small picture, it plays a twenty-second message. The picture is of my kids, and the message has them hooting and hollering. Isn't amazing how, for many, the hooting and hollering is annoying? For a Road Warrior at 2:00 A.M., two thousand miles from home, it's beautiful music.

The laptop pictures require nothing more than a scanner, or a friend with a scanner. I love looking over pictures during the low times. Everybody is smiling, and soon I'm smiling, too. Even pictures of my dogs help.

I'm not claiming these two items will cure your depression. I will say this, though. Until you know what is bothering you, it's awfully hard to repair it. My down moments are almost always related to missing my family. I leave you with these thoughts to battle your depression in Road Warrior style:

1. What's getting you down? You're listening to a writer here, but may I strongly suggest you write it down? Get a pad and write it down. Often, it isn't nearly as intimidating or daunting if you simply get it on paper and attempt to confront those ugly words.

2. If it's related to travel—and that's the single biggest source of Road Warrior depression—can you take a physical souvenir with you to lessen the depression's impact? Pictures are the obvious choice, but sometimes just a friendly pillow will do.

3. Finally—and you have to behave responsibly with this one— can you set up a reward system? Maybe it's the thought of watching a movie you taped, maybe it's a massive Cinnabun

with your name on it, waiting for your return. Whatever it is, it needs to occupy your mind and draw your focus.

Of all the lessons I present, this might be the most simplistic. Depression is a serious health problem that frequently cannot be cured by a Cinnabun. Unfortunately, most Road Warriors—like me—simply can't afford to be depressed. Our survival depends on our ability to overcome these feelings and stay sharp. It's my belief, though, that when the invading thought or thoughts are identified and exposed, it's a heck of a lot easier to design a strategy to do something about it and get it behind you.

Grief

Taking to the road can be challenging enough when things are going right at home, but what happens when they aren't? Unlike a meeting or a presentation in a conference room down the hall, a Road Warrior's meeting or presentation takes place far from home.

During my twenty years of travel, I have had plenty of bad days. I have also had some days that were painful due to a loss of someone I cared deeply for.

Wednesday, February 16th—12:15 P.M.

Tomorrow I go to work for Wells Fargo Bank to deliver a two-day seminar. I'm kind of hungry for work right now so I am raring to go. First class there and back and two nights in downtown San Francisco makes this trip somewhat appealing . . . at least for now.

The one thing that's got me a little off my game right now is the news I heard last night. I got a call around 11:00 P.M. saying that my Uncle Sam died suddenly. He had been battling a couple of problems, but was coming out of it. Then, while watching television, he died. Just like that.

Last night I had a nightmare that was loaded with symbolism regarding his passing. It was a dream that involved a sudden, senseless death. It was a small rabbit that was killed, it was brutal, it was disturbing, and it shook me up a bit. It shook me up because it was the death of my Uncle Sam.

Now I'm on my way to San Francisco and won't even be able to attend his funeral. I hate that about my job and I hate that about travel.

It's easy to say, "The show must go on." But that makes it just too easy. As I look through this entry and look at that dream, I was haunted by more than just the senseless loss of my uncle and the helplessness I felt about his passing. I was haunted by my inability to pay my respects, and although I loved him dearly, not being there for him and his family is something I will have to live with for the rest of my life.

Perspective

Perspective—there's a word I never even understood until I got married. Now I find myself overusing it a bit. "Uh, come on, honey, uh, let's keep things in perspective." As a Road Warrior, sometimes my perspective can be a bit skewed. To close this chapter on some of the emotional letdowns on the road, I think a story of a perspiring clown might be in order.

Friday, February 5th—6:25 P.M.

The day after tomorrow I have my toughest gig of the year. I pull out the "Rollo the Clown" costume and do my thing for eight six-year-olds. I'm feeling something I rarely feel . . . I'm nervous as hell.

That, my friends, is a study in perspective. Here I am, a Road Warrior who specializes in talking in front of hundreds, sometimes thousands of people for hours at a time. Eight six-year-olds had me shaking in my boots.

> **Monday, February 8th—2:00 P.M.**
> Thank goodness, my "Rollo the Clown" gig is over. I thought it went well, but I did have one small problem. I came down the stairs and was intense, perhaps too intense. Not that I scared the children, it was just I didn't slow down. I applied seminar-like energy to this gig. I ran this way and that. I not only danced around the musical chairs, falling and being silly, I danced around the kids who were eliminated from the game. We danced on the side. I took some pratfalls and really hammed it up.
>
> After about fifteen minutes, I noticed it was catching up with me. The movement, coupled with the wig, long-sleeved shirt, and short-sleeved shirt on top, began to heat me up. I started sweating rather profusely. It caused a lot of my makeup to run, but the kids didn't seem to care much. There wasn't a whole lot I could do. Even wiping my face would have been a problem, so I economized my movement, dripped for a while, and moved on.
>
> The kids seemed to like it, although I really am extremely insecure about it. Anyway, God willing, the next time Rollo (also now known as "Spitballs the Clown") makes an appearance will be for grandchildren.

Aren't moments in life like the "Spitballs the Clown" incident valuable because of their ability to remind us to keep things in perspective? To me, that was one of my most important gigs of the year for two reasons. First, it was for my youngest child. Second, it served as a good reminder of what's really important in life.

You don't have to be married to gain perspective. You just need to open your eyes, identify, and then appreciate the important things in life.

I just wish I could remember this lesson more often. Here I am, trudging about the country, fighting it out in travel and in business. A delay? A stiff neck? Oh no, my life is ruined! Late for a meeting? That's it, I want off this ride! Spend some time in the air around people you don't know and will probably never see again, and you will gain an amazing insight into the word *perspective.*

CHAPTER TWO

When the Other Team Doesn't Play Fair

It's a fact of life that not everyone you work with or socialize with will play by the rules. Many business associates, travel personnel, competitors, and others are just too busy getting by to show respect, act ethically and loyally, or otherwise do the right thing. The Road Warrior's code is simple in these situations: rise above.

I hope these lessons in playing well with others will strengthen your resolve to treat everyone you meet with honor. That's why in this chapter you'll get some interesting lessons on many who are too blinded by ego to see the truth. We had to deal with bullies when we were children on the playground. Well, often these same people grow up and become business bullies. How will you hold up to the strain of being tempted by the nagging voice crying out to do the right thing? Will you be able to stand up for yourself when it's time to say no? What about coping with the competition, and understanding the value that is a part of you? Because others are not honest, does that mean you have the right to pick your moments of trust and integrity? Let's take a look . . .

Business Bullies

In business, we come across all kinds of individuals. The ones I dislike the most are the bullies. Entering the University of Maryland at a whopping 5' 6" tall and 130 pounds, I had seen my share of bullies. Fortunately, I grew another four inches and put on about thirty pounds by the time I graduated. But I still never forgot.

Friday, March 29th—1:45 P.M.

Today's trip has me on the West Coast in Sacramento. Well, I saw him come in and it wasn't hard to spot what kind of person he was going to be. He sat in the last seat, arms folded and one leg up on the table. This was a wirehouse and I don't take any crap from these people. It's not that I am angry or mean; I just know that is the way you earn their respect. This guy came at me early, and I didn't just put him in his place, I busted him so hard that people were in tears laughing at him. I mauled him the way any good per-former who was being heckled would. The problem was, this was business, not a stand-up comedy act, and in taking him on directly, I also created a determined sniper.

We had some other run-ins, and each one got uglier. Finally, with about ten minutes to go he stuck me and stuck me good. He proclaimed to the room that none of this "touchy feely crap" would work with his clients or anyone else's. I gave an impassioned speech to control the damage of his remarks, but I lost some peo-ple. For a sniper, I had to hand it to him. His timing was impecca-ble. Although much of the class rallied around me, the momentum was gone, the energy was removed, and my sniper had gotten his revenge. He might have damaged his career, but he took me out with him.

There are a lot of bullies in business, and in the seminar busi-ness, I have seen plenty of them. Take them on directly, and you are lowering yourself to their level. I look back at that last entry and wish I had done a better job of maintaining my cool. Instead, I increased his aggression and damaged my own credibility in the opinion of everyone else who was present. To beat bullies, you don't play their game, you get them to play yours.

> **Tuesday, September 5th–11:15 P.M.**
> This was a day I would like to bottle up and save. I flew into Oklahoma City last night, woke up, started my seminar, and got nailed early by a sniper. Ah, but I was on my game. The first shot was free, but the second one wasn't. I relayed the obnoxious comment to the rest of the class and let them tell him he was wrong. That got me to our first break, and then I really went to work.
>
> I told him that I needed his help and asked him if he would talk to the group for a minute or two about the current sales system in place. He eagerly agreed. Now he was on my team. After our little talk, he spent the next hour preparing for his five minutes in the sun. Once he spoke, our relationship changed for good. He had been acknowledged in front of his peers. His ego had been soothed. All he wanted was to demonstrate that he was a person of character. He never made another sound for the next two days, without checking with me. "Our" training went well, and my bully became my best friend.

Ethics

For me, some of the most critical lessons I hope to pass on to my children are lessons that deal with ethics. I was fortunate to be tutored by my father. He taught me many things, but perhaps his greatest gift to me was the emphasis he put on ethics. Unfortunately, my father didn't have the time to parent everyone.

> **Tuesday, July 7th–7:00 A.M.**
> The person who contracted this work to be done is an ex-colleague. He now works for another corporation. I rarely discount

the programs I offer. I like to think that those who know me also know what I can do and value the other intangibles I bring to the table. The first time I taught for his new company, he demanded a discount. Since the class was local, I complied. Of course, my first discount was not deep enough, so he demanded I double it.

Now I'm set to teach another class for him. After an enormous amount of whining, he demanded an even greater discount. I agreed with the stipulation that I could put two outside customers in the training. He jumped at it. Now I've put the two outside customers in the class, and he's developed amnesia.

As only a coward and a thief would handle it, he wouldn't even speak with me by phone, he sent me e-mail. "Did you get your two trainees?" he asked.

I wrote back and told him yes.

He wrote back, "I'm looking forward to the training and of course the $2,000 more you are going to be discounting this class."

These were not paying customers I put in the class, these were people I wanted to help. Every now and then I will try to squeeze people who have little money into my programs to help them. That money issue hurt, but it truly wasn't what has me steaming. It was the careful manipulation and lies. Last year, when this person complained about costs, I sent out a complete fee structure to assure him that there are no more misunderstandings. When I told him about this, he shrugged it off as "just a document." Just a document?

Then it got worse. He sent me e-mail, of course, saying he hoped I would be able to teach this course for him and that he would hate to have to give it to someone else to teach or to cancel it. This conversation was occurring a week and a half before the training. The week was blocked for months.

Some people are ethical, and some aren't. I'm embarrassed to say that I had personally observed the long list of dissatisfied customers, consultants, and vendors that this person had abused while I was working with him. Unfortunately, my hunger for business clouded my judgment. How often have you told yourself, "This time, I'll make sure that person doesn't get the best of me." What you must learn is that these people are professionals at what they do. It's a mismatch.

> I was in his house once. It was a tour through a trophy case of companies he "had." He "had" the computer company. He "had" the roofer. He "had" the auto dealership. Each item had a proud story of how he found a loophole and got something he didn't deserve. Now I was in that trophy case.
>
> I called and tried to speak with him. I left him a voice mail saying that I did not want to discuss this by mail. If he wanted to have a meeting, fine. Although I was disappointed, the training would go on at his new price. But that wasn't enough, he had to turn the knife.
>
> He sent another e-mail saying that he was doing me a favor. Not only could he go back to Xerox and get anyone to teach this, he was paying me far too much. He told me my fees were way out of line and that he needed to tell me—as a friend—I should change my fees or I would be out of business in a year.

I would prefer not to let this get around, but I am not a litigator. Despite my anger, I put on a class to remember. Some lessons learned are not easy. In the real world, people get taken. Obviously, I have tightened up the contracts I send out, but I am also a realist. A thief is a thief. A thief will frequently be better at justifying unethical behavior than you are at upholding your ethical attempts to stop it. So then, the question that needs to be asked is this. Do you become scared and cynical from this type of behavior, which is a fact of life in business, or do you rise above it?

One of my all-time favorite customers was a group of polygraph examiners. If you're wondering what in the world a sales trainer is doing teaching sales to polygraph examiners, you're not alone. I wondered myself when they came calling.

I learned that the true job of a polygraph examiner is to extract a confession. The test might not hold up in court, but a confession will. Watching the examiners deliver these tests taught me a lot about human nature. One of the most critical lessons I learned from the confessions I was observing was this: Quite simply, it is human nature to justify improper behavior. No matter what the behavior is, we try to justify it. I watched as an embezzler, with tears in his eyes, pleaded, "It wasn't my fault, they left the safe open!"

It is amazing what we try to justify in business. Perhaps we do this so that we can stay sane at night.

Standing Up for Yourself

I'm not a person who necessarily thrives on confrontation. That's probably because in business confrontation usually means someone doesn't have the discipline to handle a situation politically. You have to rile me pretty good, and there's still only a fifty-fifty chance you'll get a rise out of me. However, when the conditions are right, I'm human, too.

Monday, May 10th—8:15 P.M.

I finished a 4:30 seminar, ran out of the room, and was on the way to the airport by 4:35. It was to be about a twenty-five-minute ride to catch a 5:15 flight. There was an accident, so it took about five minutes longer. The ticket agent could not have been nastier.

I will say I was kind of proud of myself, because I did call little Miss Nasty on her behavior. After the third remark about "Be lucky we're putting you on this flight," I did comment to her that the flight wasn't supposed to leave for another 11 minutes.

"You're a frequent flyer, you know the rules," she said in a condescending manner for all of her friends to hear.

Loudly I said, "You know what? You're not very nice, and I do know the rules, thank you! While we're going over rules, please show me the rule that says I have to listen to you continue to berate me for being stuck in traffic, running to the terminal to catch a flight, and being on time so I can get home and be with my family!!"

She backed up, almost mocking me with a hurt look and saying, "You don't think I'm nice?"

I smelled blood and responded loudly, "No, you are rude and nasty. Now, unless you feel a need to be even nastier, please, just give me my ticket." Boy, did that feel good!

I'm not advocating civil disobedience, but I am saying this: When you come across an individual who is taking delight in giving you a hard time for being a paying customer, stand up for yourself. You might even get creative about it . . .

Monday, January 10th—7:45 P.M.

Growl. Sometimes, I don't even know my own strength. I was waiting patiently in line while passenger after passenger was being treated rudely. When it was my turn, I guess I was ready to get smacked around a bit. My solution, however, was an inspiration that came to me quite spontaneously.

When I stepped up to the counter, all I wanted to do was see if I could be switched to an aisle. My not-so-friendly airline agent informed me that he wasn't going to be switching passenger seats at this time. I should come back in ten minutes. I had already waited about ten minutes in line, and couldn't figure out why he could help some, but not others. He was on a power trip.

I was heading out to conduct a sales workshop and almost forgot the tape recorders that I take with me. In a rush, I put my ten small recorders in my laptop bag, which I had hanging over my shoulder. I opened my bag, grabbed one of my little Panasonics, laid it on the counter, and politely asked him to repeat that last statement to me. That tape recorder was a magic wand. Mr. Rude became Mr. Nice. I got my aisle seat—in first class after I was upgraded.

I haven't pulled that particular stunt since, but I do carry a micro recorder with me, just in case. Fight for your rights; don't take the garbage that a few bad apples might try to shove your way. I can't promise an upgrade to first class, but I can promise that warm, satisfied feeling that comes from standing up for yourself.

Competition

In my humble opinion, competition is healthy and should be welcomed. Life is really a series of competitions. The only real danger is to make sure that when you compete, you do it fairly. You don't need to badmouth your competition to succeed. As a matter of fact, badmouthing your competition accomplishes just the opposite effect.

Thursday, November 18th–9:30 A.M.

I'm heading out of San Antonio and on to Chicago. I just completed one of the most difficult talks I have ever given in my life. During the course of two hours, I had to manage my anxiety, competitiveness, and anger.

My management of anxiety was necessary because I was trying to conduct a simulation I have taught over 100 times to smaller groups. This time, I was doing it with a large group. It started out a little rough, but it kicked into gear and miraculously worked.

My competitiveness kicked in because I followed one of the speakers I most want to crush. He doesn't have an original thought in his head, and it bothers all the professional speakers that I know. If you say it in one presentation, this guy will rip it off and say in his next presentation. In all fairness, he was at his best, actually flying in three actors from "Second City" to assist his delivery. Money is no object with this guy, and he uses his resources wisely. What he lacks in ability, he makes up for in creativity (or should I say, paying folks to be creative for him).

My anger rose when I heard the speaker in the morning. Let's just say his first name was Bill. I have seen him before, and he has seen me. He had a two-hour slot before lunch. He started his presentation with 20 minutes on the athletic event he completed the previous year and he finished with 20 minutes on the event as well. He was so pompous, so in awe of himself. As a 1983 World Ironman finisher, I can honestly say that I have not once brought it up in the past 17 years of public speaking. He clearly completed the event to make it a part of his show.

He disgusted me, but that's not what drew my anger. Once we found out how great he was, he looked at the poster of me along

the wall and mentioned what a fine speaker I was. He then pro-
ceeded to rip me apart–without referring to me by name of course,
but rather the principles I believe in. He referred to sales trainers
like me as "scab pickers." Nice.

Well, he got under my skin, and I felt a little rattled. Rule #26
of selling: "Thou shall not badmouth thy competition." The ques-
tion was, could I hold back from attacking him when I took the
stage? To attack back would bring me to his level. I had to rise
above it . . .

. . . And you know what, I almost did! When I took the stage,
the audience of 150 made no noise. Everyone seemed to be curi-
ous about what I would do. I decided to get it over with early
so we could get to work, so I made one and only one reference
to how I felt. I simply said, "I am Rob Jolles, and I am a scab
picker." The crowd burst out in cheers and applause and some
even rose to their feet. I thanked them profusely and went about
my task.

In a way, I got lucky. The crowd's response reminded me that I didn't need to go any further to rise above the situation. Normally, I fly out right after a talk, but I hung around after this one and spent an extra night out. Senior management cornered me at the bar, bought me a drink, stuck a cigar in my mouth, apologized, and assured me that the speaker in question would never be used again. They slapped me on the back and called me their favorite scab picker. It's not a nickname I would like to encourage, but for that night in my life, I kind of liked it.

For a Road Warrior, competition is just another fact of life. Every trip matters, and for me, every presentation matters. I do not pick my spots for when I plan on "turning it on." I welcome the competition because I am conditioned to cope effectively with it. Compete with yourself. Ultimately that's the competition that counts most.

Value

Working for any corporation creates scars. Some are good scars, and some, well, you would just as soon try and forget about them. One of the good scars I received from my days at Xerox involved the concept of value.

People typically expect to hear two things when they meet with Xerox. First, whatever they are looking at will be top quality. Second, it won't be inexpensive.

Tuesday, January 20th—4:15 P.M.

I have just landed in Chicago and am in a limo on my way into the city, or the Loop, as it is called here. I will be teaching a two-day school for a customer from whom I haven't heard in a while—First Chicago Bank.

At one point, they were one of my largest customers. Then another corporation started copying Xerox sales training programs, and good-bye business! It was not my responsibility to patrol these customers, although I yelled loud and long for Xerox to do something about this.

Of course, the question is, how did another training outfit knock Rob Jolles out? They made the customer an offer they just couldn't refuse. They offered the training for free!

As the story has now been communicated to me, their sales numbers have fallen, morale is down, and the program has failed.

Now, almost two years later, they're back. This time, they want to belly up to the bar again and pay for their training. They got what they had been paying for. Nothing.

As a good little Xeroid, I was taught to introduce my customers to the term *T.C.O.* (Total Cost of Ownership). When a customer would complain and say to us, "That costs too much," our response was always the same. "By cost, are you referring to the cost of purchasing this product or the cost of owning this product?" They usually asked, "Huh? What are you talking about?" We explained that we simply wanted customers to consider *all* of the costs associated with the decisions they were making. We were teaching lessons in value.

Strangely enough, I'm willing to bet that this is not a new lesson to you, my reader. The inexpensive roofer, painter, and auto mechanic have burned us all, and the list goes on and on. It isn't the lesson I am concerned about, it's the shelf life of the lesson. In other words, we lose sight of value to get ourselves a "bargain." We ultimately pay for it and get burned. We swear we won't make that mistake again. We don't . . . for the next six months to a year, and then we make the same mistake all over again. Whether it's looking for bargains in travel or in business, please, go with your instincts. You truly get what you pay for.

Trust

For years, I have been presenting a negotiation skills simulation that teaches many lessons. Perhaps my favorite lesson deals with trust. The simulation invites betrayal. Betrayal invites emotion, a trainer's dream.

Friday, November 22nd—5:00 P.M.

Traveling to Dallas this week has given me a new lesson to add to my list. I learned over these last two days that the trainer I have paid to conduct the seminar with me is a formidable opponent— but not much of a team player. He is a pretty good trainer and a shameful promoter. He came into my room schmoozing with my students. He schmoozed with my business contacts and schmoozed with the customer decision makers. I'm disappointed.

The problem is, I'm not sure people can see through this in two days. It is not how I do business and I don't like it. "Let me sit next to you at dinner." "Let me buy you all some drinks." "Let me get that for you." I respect his attempts at selling, but these are my customers.

I had to stay up late last night, because this trainer wanted to party with the class. It's unprofessional, but if one instructor does it, it makes anyone who doesn't look like a stick-in-the-mud.

I will perform my own damage control with the customers for whom he was taking business cards, but I have learned. I did a great job teaching my class, and although I didn't dance with them (guess who did), I believe I earned their respect. This seminar cost the trainer I was using a great deal of money, because he will never teach another one for my company.

Once trust is broken, it's very difficult, if not impossible, to repair. This is a business lesson that is usually learned best by having trust broken. In my years in business, I have seen business relationships survive under the most difficult circumstances, but a betrayal of trust is nearly impossible to survive.

Want an example of how trust is betrayed on a daily basis? Look at the airlines and how they handle their problems. Never is this more evident than in a Road Warrior's confrontation with the most depressing and heinous word that can ever be uttered: *delays* (an honorary four-letter word if ever there was one). That's the enemy in the world of the Road Warrior and one we dread seeing or hearing. There are few things that can turn a good trip sour more quickly than that dreaded delay. That, and of course, lack of communication!

In fact, every now and then, I have to question myself on how ridiculously confident I am when it comes to flying.

Wednesday, August 12th–8:30 P.M.

We've been moved to the penalty box, which is the Road Warrior's term for holding area while we await a visit from maintenance. I don't know what it is, but for goodness sake, we were fit enough to leave the gate–let's just go!

I refuse to believe there can be a problem. I'll tell you how trusting I am. From time to time, the pilot will get on and make an announcement like, "Ladies and gentlemen, we have a light coming on indicating that one of our engines might not be cooling properly. It may very well be a bad sensor, but we're going to call maintenance and have them take a quick look at it."

Here comes the sick part. My reaction is to want to shout, "Oh, come on. Chances are it's a faulty sensor. We're not really having a problem with our engine. Please, let's push off and go! We've got two engines, anyway." Yes, I'm glad they checked out that sensor, but I can assure you, I'm not the only Road Warrior with these thoughts.

7:30 P.M.

I'd rather have this happen on the way out than the way back, but "Houston, we have a problem." A lot of storms are in the area, and a doozy has just hit Charlotte. My connection just diverted to some town I've never heard of. With my travel schedule, I assure you its unusual to encounter a small town that I have not heard of. The plane is being refueled and is supposed to come here . . . eventually. With the lightning, heavy rain, and general ugliness it looks like I won't be getting in until late. Then I need to get up early for another grueling eight hours of selling fun. The best guess from the counter person is that my 8:15 flight might get in around 10:00.

A nice lesson is unfolding before our eyes involving trust. Let's make sure we learn from it. You are connecting from a major airport and heading to a smaller airport. Weather is affecting the airport where you are and your destination. You may not know it, and the airlines aren't going to tell you, but you are in significant trouble.

How do you think they determine which flights get canceled? Yep, it's the smaller planes heading to the smaller airports, with the smaller passenger revenues. It's business—an ugly business.

11:45 P.M.

Liars, liars, liars. Now I know why some call this airline "Useless Air." They promised a flight and had us wait for a flight that was never going to arrive. By doing this, they eliminated our chances to hop on another carrier. The flight is canceled, and after I wait in a line for a good half hour, I get a room in an airport hotel (horrible as usual) and wait for tomorrow.

Travel will teach you a lot about trust. Dr. Frank Crane once said of trust, "You may be deceived if you trust too much, but you will live in torment unless you trust enough." In travel or in business, this Catch-22 plays itself out on a regular basis. In the real world, trust is often not an option but thrust upon us. It's what you do with the information you receive and how you react to it that separates the true Road Warriors from the masses.

Integrity

Is there a more important lesson in life to learn than to aspire to be a person of integrity? The following story goes back to my early journal days, but it may contain the seeds of the most important lesson I've learned—don't give in to the pressure to lie.

Thursday, February 21st–7:55 P.M.

I am emotionally shot. Today is a day I will never forget for the rest of my life. I have to backtrack to about six months ago. One of my largest customers came here to Xerox to discuss rolling out a training program to banks. They wanted to use our materials and our trainers. We wanted to get a development fee and a percentage of every delivery. Sounded good to me.

Once the numbers were set, we brought in an outside development consultant and went to work. Over the last six months, I got very close to our customer. It is the biggest sales training program I ever put together, and at the risk of sounding corny, I was literally moved by the amount of trust they put in me. Through these six months, they have never questioned the decisions I made, because, as they told me so often, they trusted me.

It has been a difficult six months for me, because of the diverse personalities with whom I have been working.

- First, there is the customer. With a lot of time, money, and potential market share invested, and with their industry on the line, they want this project done right.
- Next, there's the consulting company we are using. Their motivation is income generated. They estimated their costs months ago and overruns mean losses in income for them. They want this project done well, but done right the first time.
- Next, there are my bosses at Xerox. They looked to me to make estimates as well. To put it bluntly, they expect me to turn a profit—a good one.
- Finally, there's me. I am the liaison between what has frequently felt like all of the warring parties.

Well, today we launched our masterpiece in a pilot format at the customer's site. All the warring parties attended. Make no mistake about it, these parties were officially warring. The delivery was a bit late, which upset the customer. Extra time had to be put into the project, which upset the consultant and the Xerox bosses. Not only was I there as a peace negotiator, I was also the trainer to deliver this all-day pilot.

I felt pretty confident that the program was going to get rave reviews—except for one small area. The customer had paid $20,000 for a video that was to be shot in a bank, showing an investment rep selling to a customer. A decision was made to hire an actor, and I'm not sure where we found our actor, but this guy was terrible. After a video shoot that went about twice as long as we would *have liked, the editing crew claimed they had enough to piece together a good video. It never happened, and the video was weak. The "powers that be" made it clear we weren't going through this again. The video was "good enough." I was told if the customer complained bitterly, we would reshoot it.*

The class was delivered, the feedback was collected, and we sat down to talk about it. The feedback from the participants was strong except for one area . . . the video. The customer asked the consultant what he thought of the video. "It's terrific!" he said. The customer seemed a bit perplexed and asked the Xerox team at the table what we thought. "Works well," they said.

There was an eerie silence. The customer seemed confused. It sure looked like the emperor had no clothes, but all the pros were telling them that the emperor looked just great. Then the customer looked at me. "What do you think, Rob?"

That entry was made almost thirteen years ago. I remember it as if it was yesterday. I remember it, because I was scared. My business classes at the University of Maryland had never prepared me for the events that were unfolding. I was a Xerox employee, and if I stood for nothing else in my life, I stood for loyalty. The problem was, loyal to whom? The customer? My company? Whose side was I on? Looking back on this event in my life, I was fortunate. I could not have provided the customer with a better answer.

I froze. As an aspiring professional speaker, I am embarrassed to say I couldn't think of anything to say. The customer saw everything he needed to see. He claimed he was thirsty and wanted to take a break. The customer then asked if he could see me for a minute.

We went into a side room and he asked me again what I thought of the video. I stammered around a bit and he made it easy on me. He basically told me what to say. "It isn't very good, is it?" he said. I had a little trouble making eye contact, but I finally found a few words. "No, it's not very good at all."

Our private meeting ended right there. We walked back into the larger meeting room and sat down. My customer announced that the program was good, but the video was unacceptable. It would have to be reshot. I didn't look up, but I was getting some pretty serious looks from my bosses at Xerox. We packed up and headed for the parking lot.

Surprisingly, it wasn't my bosses who were the first to attack me in the parking lot, it was the consultant.

"We have a Judas amongst us," he sneered. The attacks began and were relentless. It was painfully obvious what happened, and there was no way to deny it. I had turned on my own team.

I felt the best defense was a good offense. "Whatever happened to our commitment to our customer?" I snapped back. "Whatever happened to integrity?" A shouting match continued until my Xerox counterparts mercifully put a stop to it. It was over, but it was a long trip home.

In a sense, so was my corporate career. After a long and prosperous association with Xerox, six months later, I left to head out on my own. I was disillusioned, and perhaps so were they. In fact, I had cost my company $20,000—the cost to shoot that video and, in my opinion, shoot it right. To me, it didn't matter whether the customer figured this out on their own or not. They trusted me.

The program was a tremendous success. When I left Xerox, this customer called me, never having forgotten what happened that day in the side room. To this day, over a decade later, he remains one of my closest friends in business, and his company is one of my most loyal clients. Given the chance to relive that moment in my life with all those warring parties, I wouldn't change a thing. It was the right thing to do.

Sometimes, doing the right things does not net the results you are looking for. In my mind, acting with integrity means doing what's right, regardless of the outcome.

Friday, September 6th–5:00 P.M.

I'm in a pretty good mood. I have finished my series of five one-day seminars for a pharmaceutical company. This has kept me busy over the last two weeks, but they're over now. They also made me a great deal of money.

These people are struggling. It made me a little sad. I always knew these people as one of the happiest companies I ever worked with. Now, they're one of the most depressed. They feel management sold them out on an acquisition that just occurred. They are overworked and underpaid. They have too many products and cover territories that are too large. Their goals have been set too high, and worst of all, their customer service support is terrible. Many are seeking work elsewhere.

I am not ignoring these problems, however. I have written a letter to senior management outlining what I have seen and heard. It most likely will infuriate senior management that a consultant took it upon himself to criticize their company, but I don't care. My heart says I need to write this letter, and I have. I will send it tomorrow.

The people of this company have been very good to me over the years. I owe it to them. I told a few people about the letter and they were quite emotional. They couldn't believe I would basically commit professional suicide within this account to get their message heard. In fact, it's not that difficult a decision. It's what a person with integrity would do. I'm just pleased that these types of decisions are becoming easier and easier to make.

The letter tells it like it is and offers some suggestions. These are not solutions I can help them with, but I did recommend that they talk with people who could help. The letter might be preachy, but it will be hard to ignore.

I never heard from any of the four senior managers after sending that letter. In fact, mysteriously my work for this company ended abruptly. After four years of consulting work—and well over six figures in consulting fees—I would not hear back from this company for another four years . . .

February 1st–1:00 A.M.

What a day! I'm heading back from a trip to the West Coast where I just nailed a fantastic seminar for an old friend . . .

A number of years ago I fell out of favor with senior management for sticking up for the people in the field. Well, the senior management has moved on, and the people in the field have moved up. They never forgot me, and they want me back to do extensive work with them. I really like the people I'm working with, and they like me.

To this day, that pharmaceutical company remains one of my favorite customers. They were well worth the wait.

CHAPTER THREE

Deals and Dealers

After dealing with internal issues and the need to be who you say you are, it's time to look at what business you are traveling for and what people you are traveling to see. It's difficult to conduct business without being sensitive to the individuals you'll be dealing with and the lessons they will teach a Road Warrior. In this chapter, I focus on keeping your business priorities in the right order.

Here then, I would like to present a new series of lessons that focus on the people side of business. What sort of deals are you prepared to make? What lessons in business and life can be derived from your adherence to customer service, and what can be learned in negotiation from time spent on the road? Is it realistic to count on being able to love *all* of your customers, and if not, how will this impact you as a Road Warrior? Finally, when you take to the road, particularly the international road, how will you cope with and embrace the cultural differences that are bound to demand your attention?

Deals

Remember in the game Monopoly when you made a trade and later regretted it? You couldn't go back and fix it because "a deal is a deal." It isn't uncommon to have second thoughts about a deal that may very well have been struck in a moment of weakness. Too bad; a deal is a deal.

Friday, July 5th–10:30 P.M.

I'm on the road and on my way out to teach a class for a customer, and my mood is not good. Four months ago, this customer called my office, and all I can say is, their timing was excellent. In my business, I book out approximately two to three months in advance. This is the life of a professional speaker.

Every November things slow down. Thanksgiving through Christmas, as with most businesses, other than a few year-end meetings, business grinds to a halt. What's worse, the next year's calendar slows as well. Now, after eight years, you would think I would simply trust that calendar to fill back up again, but I have to wait for January, and I get a little nervous.

I got the call for this one in November for a seminar delivery in February. The customer didn't have a lot of money, but I jumped at it anyway. In January, I got another call from a very hungry customer.

"We really need you," they said. When I told them I was booked, they offered to double my fee. I swallowed hard.

Too often in business, we make deals we learn to regret. It happens in professional sports all the time. Sometimes these mistakes favor management. Sometimes these mistakes favor the athlete. All in all, it would be my guess that these mistakes probably come out even.

One thing I've never understood is why an athlete would decide to renegotiate his contract. Help me out here. A deal has been struck. I would assume the athlete's performance has exceeded expectations, and now he feels the deal is no longer fair. In the history of professional sports, I can't recall one instance of management wanting to renegotiate a contract due to expectations that have not been met.

I am in no way a friend of management. I gave it a shot once at Xerox and was miserable. I just believe that in business, a deal is a deal. If ever I was fortunate enough to own a sports team, I'd like to think I would be fair owner. I will tell you this, however. If I ever had an agent come in to renegotiate a contract, I would place two phone calls. The first would be to the athlete to make sure this request represented his personal wishes. The second would be to whatever media source could get the word out the fastest that the athlete in question was now in a position to be traded.

> I placed a call to the client with whom I was booked. Before I could open my mouth, the customer thanked me. They told me they knew the deal I had offered them was for a reduced rate. They told me how much they enjoy hearing me speak. This presentation would be the fourth time I would be speaking at their annual kick-off meeting.
>
> Thoughts of the other deal that had been offered to me raced through my head. My greed took a back seat, though. I had made a deal, and a deal is a deal.

It would be a better story if I could finish it by telling you how much more business I received from this client, or how I was able to juggle the other client and grab the big bucks that were on the table. Neither story would be true, and that's why it belongs in this lesson. A deal is a deal. Not when it's convenient for you, or there

is the promise of a better deal down the line. A deal is a deal . . .
period.

Customer Service

Every business seems to grapple with the concept of customer service. If you ask me, there is never a genuinely good deal without it.
Want a lesson in watching an industry that still doesn't understand
the concept of customer service? On the next flight you take, shell
out the extra bucks, or cash those upgrades in and go sit in first
class.

> ### Tuesday, April 27th–9:00 A.M.
> I'm sitting in first class and stewing a bit. It's that ridiculous first
> class meal policy that has me fuming. There were three meal selec-
> tions today. The first choice was the wonderful filet mignon. Oh
> boy, that sounded good. We have three rows of first class seats.
> That choice was out before they hit the second row.
>
> Next was a wonderful chicken breast. Perhaps it was the five
> seminars I sold today, but I really had a meat craving. Still, we can't
> always get what we want in life. Chicken it was . . . until they ran
> out of the that choice in the second row. Nope, when they got to
> me in the third row, I was offered the turkey mush. I chose the
> pasta from coach, instead.
>
> They don't seem the least bit sorry or remorseful. In fact, they
> should be ashamed of themselves.

I want to prepare you for a little Jolles whining here, so if
you need to leave the room and come back, I should be done in
a paragraph or two. The meal choice policy has to be one of the

stupidest airline policies of all and I am dumbfounded that they can't figure out how angry it makes the passengers!

Imagine for a moment that you run a business. By some lucky stroke, you are able to section off your customers who are most willing to pay full price and beyond for your services. All you really have to do is make them happy. The airlines just don't get it. Allow me one more "First Class Food Tale":

Wednesday, August 16th—7:30 P.M.

Now, on the nuttier side of Rob Jolles's existence, I have made an official statement on this flight. I'm sitting in first class in Delta, and of course, they ran out of the good meal well before they got to me. I am now an official martyr.

I just stared into the stewardess's eyes when she said "no crab cakes" and waited for her to blink. It took a few seconds, but of course, she did offer me the other meal. I told her I wanted nothing.

Now, I've done this before, but this time I went a step further in my "martyrhood." I wrote a little note. On that note I wrote the following:

> *"I came around 2A, where Mr. Rob Jolles was sitting. When I informed him that we were out of the first class meal he wanted, he refused all service from that moment further. Maybe he did this because this was the third straight flight we have been out of his selection. Maybe he did this because he's one of the only passengers up here in first class who paid a full first class fare, and was not upgraded into this cabin. That means he probably paid at least $500 more than anyone else we gave his meal away to. Maybe, just maybe, he was sick and tired of us adhering to a policy that promotes failure."*

When I gave it to her, I told her that I did not hold her responsible in the slightest way for this problem, and was not angry with her at all. She was relieved, confided in me that she gets hassled for this airline issue all the time, and not only signed the note, encouraged me to send it to Delta.

I did send that note to Delta, and as I had predicted, they sent me back a free upgrade certificate. I called them and asked if they had any intentions of changing their meal policies for first class. They told me no, but said they were sorry and hoped the upgrade would make everything OK. I then ripped the upgrade up while on the phone so my customer service rep could hear it. I told them I was sorry too, and would do all in my power to not fly that airline until the policy was changed. My theory is, if you are going to be a martyr, you might as well go all the way.

Well, they must have been listening, because Delta, and a couple of the other airlines have changed their policy . . . kind of . . .

Monday, January 29th–7:30 P.M.

Hey, they're out of meals in first class! Imagine that? However, I will say they've disappointed their customers in a new and creative way. I moved up to get near the front of the first class cabin, and Delta outsmarted me again. Seems that they now alternate between starting from the front or the back depending on whether it's an odd or even numbered flight. Brilliant. Now they can disappoint their customers on an equal basis.

I've now seen United go so far as working down one side of the cabin, starting at the front again, and working down the other side of the cabin. I guess this is to confuse us at a higher level to make triply sure that no one knows whether they are getting their meal or not. There's a lot of thought going into not delivering what you promise to your best customers.

Wednesday, November 29th–7:30 A.M.

Here's something new—they ran out of meals in first class! Ah, but this story has an interesting twist. Sitting in row two, I thought I had it made. It was either have the ten pound cheese omelet with airline sausage (very scary), or a fruit plate with cereal. When I was given the bad news about running out of the fruit plate, I asked, "How does that happen without even getting out of row one?" Amazingly enough, I was told there was only one fruit plate loaded on the plane.

The story should end there, but it doesn't. Get this. That one meal didn't even go to a passenger. The stewardess slipped up and told me that the pilot didn't want the cereal portion of this break-fast meal and asked if I wanted it. She then put her hand over her mouth and turned red. Of course, I asked her. "Are you telling me that the only fruit plate on the menu you handed us went to the pilot?" She nodded and looked quite embarrassed.

We finished with my usual speech. "I'm not blaming you, but for $1,800, one-way, I would think you would have a few more meals . . . for the passengers!" When will they learn?

We're not talking about a ticket that is a few dollars more than coach. We're talking about a ticket that is hundreds if not *thousands* more than coach. I'm praying that an airline will read this message and get the point. If you have twelve first class passengers, bring thirty-six *frozen* meals aboard. Microwave the ones your passengers are paying a thousand dollars each for and save the rest for the next flight or better yet, give them to the nearest homeless shelter.

Customer service is not a slogan or sales pitch. It's a culture that is either adopted and adhered to by an organization, or not. You can't be "somewhat" interested in customer service, and you can't pick your spots. The airlines have never learned this particular lesson, nor do they seem to be in any hurry to learn this lesson. If you're running a business, however, make sure you get this one memorized. Remember, as they say, if you don't take care of your best customers, someone else will.

Negotiation

Whenever you hear anyone lecture on negotiation skills, you always hear the same thing. "The goal is to create a win-win agreement." How lovely. As a matter of fact, I couldn't agree with it more. The only problem is that this mythical agreement frequently doesn't represent reality.

Tuesday, November 17th–8:10 P.M.

I am in the process of trying to establish a relationship with a large office supply company. This will be my opportunity to prove myself. Unfortunately, this company is not used to paying my kind of rates. They did come up considerably from where they started, but we are still a bit light. They will come up more if this program is as good as I say it is. Nothing like adding a little pressure to one's life.

In the negotiations, I ended up setting a delivery fee with a cap on travel. However, we agreed that whatever surplus there was on *travel, they would use to buy books. I drove up here to eliminate the airfare and buy them books with the savings. They seemed quite impressed that I believed in my program as much as I do.*

So, here I sit, having eaten at McDonald's to save on food, with my car outside to save on airfare, and staying in a cheap Holiday Inn to save on hotel expenses. I'm kind of slumming it right now.

With this company and occasionally other companies I work with, I took a classic lose-win approach to negotiations. This approach simply suggests that one side is willing to take a loss to try to ensure that the next time around, they will not take a loss again.

It's a little like watching a basketball game. I happen to be a big fan, since I played and coached the sport and have witnessed this scenario in games many times. Watch for it yourself. Watch as the referee blows his whistle and calls a player for walking. Moments later, an irate coach comes shooting off the bench to protest.

"What are you, blind?" he screams. "You've got to be out of your mind! There's no way he dragged that pivot foot!"

Now I've watched a lot of games, and I've got to tell you, I've never seen a referee answer back with this response: "You know, the more you speak, Coach, the more you make sense. I didn't really get a good look at it anyway. Come to think of it, *he didn't* walk! Thanks for the help."

Why then would a coach go through this charade? Quite simply, he's looking for what's referred to in basketball as a "makeup call." The next time you watch a game, watch how quickly a mysterious call seems to go against the team that just benefited from the call in question. What the coach is really saying is, "I'll give you this one if you give me the next one." This scenario is played out frequently in life, and it represents an intelligent approach to negotiation.

Loving (Most) Customers

When I first went into business I was told in no uncertain terms, "You must love your customer." Sometimes it was tough love, but just the same, I practiced what was preached to me. As I matured in business, however, I learned this is not always possible.

I recognize that probably sounds a bit heartless, but I want to deal with the real world of business and not the fantasy world. I have come to peace with the belief that in business, we are often nothing more than mercenaries fighting wars we are paid to wage. In the past, I would look at customers and think to myself, "that one I want to work for, and that one I don't." Now, I find myself saying, "that one I want to work for and negotiate with, and that one I don't want to work with so I won't negotiate." It may not be politically correct, but it's a lesson I've learned just the same.

Of course, the "don't negotiate" rule can sometimes land you some business you wish you did not have. At full price, however, it is easier to grin and bear it.

Friday, March 20th—7:15 A.M.

For the last couple of years, I have encountered a guy at a number of high-level bank meetings whom I really don't like. He is hypocritical and boring. What's more, he loves to lecture everyone on how they should live their lives, which coincidently is the way he lives his life. The best analogy I could use for this guy is that he sometimes reminds me of a male Cathy Lee Gifford. Yuck!

A key contact of mine asked me to help their company get more business from his bank. My skin crawled, but I worked so hard to get along with this guy, I'm now his buddy. Anyway, he has invited me to speak at his sales rally today, and when I sent him a proposal at top dollar, he accepted. So here I am.

Now my Cathy Lee clone has made some changes that are really turning my stomach. He persuaded me to stay on later and talked me into helping him with a project he is working on. That has now escalated into a request to do his presentation with him. I'm pretty sure I can survive this mess, but I tell you, a knuckle-head is a knucklehead is a knucklehead.

Road Warriors take to the road to do business. Sometimes it's business we like, and sometimes it's business we don't like. The most important thing is to take a look at the big picture and determine whether you want to fill that suitcase and take the trip. If the decision is to go, get ready to show love. As for me, after forcing myself to stomach these types of situations, my greatest joy is creating that invoice!

Bridging Cultural Differences

Before I leave the topic of making deals, I want to emphasize how bridging cultural gaps will give you an advantage. The Road Warriors who never leave their hometown even when on the road won't stand a chance against the ones who reach out to other cultures. Cultural opportunities are all around us. When you are lucky enough to take your Road Warrior act out of the country, keep your eyes open. Sometimes it can be as simple as a cab ride. Of course, you'll never take that cab ride if you don't leave your hotel.

Sunday, June 23rd–8:00 P.M.

My first trip to Egypt, and I am so excited! I can't believe it. I'm traveling with another trainer from Xerox. As Dorothy once said, "I don't think we're in Kansas anymore, Toto!"

We stayed in Cairo for a week and a half. During that time, I sat by the Nile, ate Egyptian food every night (it became easier to simply ask them not to tell me what I was eating), smoked tobacco from an Egyptian water pipe, rode horseback up to the Pyramids, and basically bathed myself in every cultural experience I could.

Wednesday, June 26th–10:00 P.M.

I feel like I have really gotten to know Cairo. Last night I got to experience perhaps the greatest challenge of all. I asked if I could drive. For anyone who has ever been to Cairo, I don't need to tell you what a challenge that is. For those who have not, let's just put it this way. The only rule for driving in Cairo is, "There are no rules!" It was a challenge, and one that my Egyptian friends claimed no other American they had invited had ever taken.

My Egyptian friends were bursting with pride as they boasted about how they converted me into a citizen of Cairo. When we left Cairo, my Egyptian friends hugged me and became emotional.

That trip occurred thirteen years ago. A handful of other Xerox trainers took the same trip, hid in their rooms, and have never been invited back. I was invited back as a Xerox employee the next year. I have been invited back four times since I left Xerox. To this day, these are my friends, and Cairo is my adopted city. Not bad for a Jewish kid from Maryland. As Vincent Van Gogh once said, "What would life be like if we didn't have the courage to attempt anything?"

CHAPTER FOUR

Workflow

Go? Or No Go?

The road can humble anyone, regardless of your experience or stamina. In business, much like sport, it's easy enough to be up when you're up, but what happens when you're down? There is a ticket with your name on it, and this ticket has no feelings. It could care less how you are doing today or who you are seeing.

The lessons found in this chapter are dedicated to the question of workflow. How will you react to that voice in your head that says, "quit"? When should you listen to it and obey? If you are unable to generate business, there will be no workflow to worry about, so how will you perform to maximize these trips you take? Finally, what about the great equalizers in business: hard work and hustle? To go, or not to go—that's the question . . .

Not Quitting

One of my fondest memories as a kid was watching movies late at night with my dad. One of my favorite movies was a film called *Cool Hand Luke*. I had no idea until later in life just how important that movie was to me. Nobody can ever forget the boxing scene where Paul Newman's staggering character just won't stay down. I may not look like Paul Newman, but I admire Luke's spirit.

Monday, February 2nd—12:35 P.M.
Chicago is usually a little kinder to me. I felt out of rhythm on this presentation. I guess I had been riding a series of good ones, so I

was due to have one not be quite as good, and this one was it. I moved, I sweat, I bellowed, and I sweat some more. They just weren't the most animated audience, and it took its toll on me.

My timing was off, as well. The guy who was running the meeting is someone with whom I have worked in the past. He is a time nut, and so am I. I said some things that were unnecessary, left out some things I really wanted to say, and fought the clock the whole way to get it down to an hour.

Ah. But I don't finish an entry without looking at the positives. When I sweat, and I sweat a lot on this one, I know I'm working hard. I wasn't flat, and everyone there knew I was giving it my all. Sometimes, that's the best asset a speaker has, because what I lacked in rhythm, I made up for in energy. That's what I'll take from this talk today, and that will give me comfort and confidence to get this one behind me and push on. I never gave up!

By not quitting, Cool Hand Luke won. The outcome was secondary. I am reminded of a quote I saw once that I have up in my office.

Here I lie, beaten, but not slain. I lie down to bleed a while, but will rise, to fight again.

As a kid, I was always the shortest person in my class. Ironically, I fell in love with the game of basketball, which does not cater to small people. Just the same, what I lacked in size, I made up for in determination. I was Cool Hand Luke, and I wasn't coming out of that circle and quitting. I tried out for many basketball teams and made far fewer than I tried for, but I never stopped trying. Five root canals, three teeth knocked out, a broken ankle, a broken wrist, and countless broken fingers, but I tried.

In college, I fell in love with distance running because to me, a distance race was nothing more than a test of not quitting. My first race was a half marathon, and my next was a marathon. Soon I was moving into triathlons, and ultra-distance events.

To this day, I still love to test my simple desire to not quit. From swimming in from Alcatraz on the West Coast to swimming across the Chesapeake Bay on the East Coast, I love the simple challenge of not quitting.

I know I'm not alone. Consider some of these famous individuals, whose names you know. What you might not realize is that you know them simply because they wouldn't quit.

- Ray Kroc was fifty-two years old when he began the business we know as McDonald's.

- Thomas Edison was rumored to have failed close to fifty thousand times before he achieved the results he was looking for in his pursuit of his new storage battery. When a reporter questioned the number of experiments necessary to achieve results, Edison remarked, "Results?" "Why, I have gotten a lot of results. I know fifty thousand things that won't work."

- Harland Sanders was sixty-five when he launched Kentucky Fried Chicken.

- Theodor Geisel's first book was turned down by twenty-eight publishers before Vanguard finally accepted it. After that Geisel went on to write forty-six other books, including two that you're sure to recognize: *The Cat in the Hat* and *Green Eggs and Ham*. We know him by his pen name, Dr. Seuss.

Quitting

Now that I have done a decent job of explaining my belief in not quitting, let me oil up the other side of my mouth and make a legitimate case *for* quitting. Think back for a moment, and try and remember the last time you changed jobs. What did you feel? What drove you to that decision? How emotional was it for you? Sometimes, our blinding determination not to give up can cloud our judgment and provide false hope.

When I left Xerox, it was extremely emotional for me. After all, who leaves Xerox? I grew up watching my dad and believing that work consisted of doing what you were told for twenty-five years and receiving a gold watch for your troubles. If you were loyal to the corporation, the corporation would be loyal to you.

It's a wonderful fantasy, but is this the picture of corporate life you intend to pass on to your children? Personally, I would think twice, because I don't believe it represents reality in today's world. What's more, I don't think the corporation wants you to feel this way, either.

You see, much like marriage partners, Xerox and I had both changed. I had certain needs they could no longer fulfill, and they had certain needs I no longer wanted to fulfill. Neither one of us wanted to say good-bye. When I even whispered to my friends that I was considering leaving the corporation, I was greeted with gasps and moans.

In the spring of 1993, I left Xerox Corporation. In a sense, I tried to stay, but it just didn't work out. I had nervously handed Xerox an ultimatum and they responded, "No." We did not argue or fight. There was no bad blood, and in fact, they became one of my first consulting customers. They did me a tremendous favor. They treated me with compassion. By turning down my "demands" they told me clearly, "Don't work here anymore."

I will always be grateful that they were as blunt as they were. To this day, I frequently witness corporate marriages gone bad with neither party truly confronting the other. In fact, both the worker and the corporation seem to bathe in the bad blood between them.

I know that many of you who read this have confronted the depression that follows. We question ourselves. What went wrong? Where did I fail? Well I'm here to tell you, nothing went wrong. In my opinion, it is simply a natural progression we all go through.

Yes, it might be natural, but it is still frightening. When the business marriage ends, we are forced to face perhaps the single biggest fear that hangs ominously above us all. That fear is a fear of change.

This next entry is very meaningful to me. It was written on a balcony overlooking the ocean in North Carolina right before I left my safe haven at Xerox. It is dedicated to anyone who has left or is considering leaving a safe but unfulfilling environment. It is also dedicated to those who want to go out on their own or challenge their boundaries. This one even has a title to it.

Tuesday, May 5th–8:00 P.M.: "Leaving the Womb"

What separates success from failure? Could it be the conquering of fear or the paralysis of avoiding fear?

As I sit in another hotel room contemplating my future, I am at a crossroads in my career. I know now what I must do, yet I find myself fearing the mere thought of a dream I have pursued for so long. The question is, Why? Looking out over the ocean, I think I have finally figured it out.

The wire I find myself looking over has never been raised higher in the air. To say there is no net beneath is a cop-out. Deep in my soul I do believe that I can financially survive such a fall. What I now realize is that what I truly fear is the emotional fall.

"Be careful what you wish for, you might just get it." What a haunting phrase this has turned out to be. It is so unlike me to dwell on the negative, especially when I have so much that is positive to focus on. It is futile to rationalize my decision. It almost becomes tiring to hear how right the time to leave is and how wrong the current situation is. This is not news to me, anymore. This is a lesson I have learned.

What is the worst thing that will happen to me if I am not successful? Could it possibly be worse than what will happen to me if I do not have the courage to try? My talent is apparent. It is my courage that is untried. It is now time to test that courage.

I am not preaching to anyone to leave their company. I am simply saying to those who see the writing on the wall, trust your instincts. The same principle applies to just about any decision that requires significant change. Ask almost anyone around you who has left these types of difficult situations, and they will recite these words like a mantra: "I can't believe I waited so long." I hope these words give you courage to face your fears.

Generating Business

The life of a consultant is an interesting one. If a company ever invented calendars that contained only two months, my trainers and I would snap them up. In fact, for many whose business depends on selling (and that also covers most of us who are in business for ourselves), it is unusual to be able to generate business more than two to three months in advance. That's where creative prospecting comes into play.

My business allows me to study many other businesses. With a clientele of almost two hundred different companies—and more than a hundred of them Fortune 500 companies—I have witnessed one of the oldest lessons in business played out again and again. I am referring to the 80-20 rule.

As a reminder, the 80-20 rule states that 80 percent of business usually comes from 20 percent of the clients. Oh, I know, a lot of professors will lecture the business community about how dangerous that can be to a business, but these are tenured professors who are not competing actively in the real world.

I embrace the 80-20 rule. I see it as an opportunity. Everyone in business has key clients that are critical to them. Properly nurtured and taken care of, these clients can significantly strengthen a person's business. Yes, we never stop trying to garner new clients and turn them into critical clients, but this lesson is about fighting with all your might to hold on. Well, I'm a salesman, but I think it's time to admit I don't sell all of my clients all of the time. Sometimes, it just doesn't work out that well. The client just doesn't want to employ my services. If a company doesn't want you at their year-end meeting, there is just no opportunity . . . or is there?

Wednesday, December 16th–4:15 P.M.

Last business trip of the year, and ironically, I will not be conducting any training. This falls into the category of damage control. I am in New York to spend tomorrow with one of my former best customers. The relationship has been deteriorating for quite some time, and hopefully, I will emerge with a better understanding of their direction.

After an assault of persuasion, I was invited to this meeting, but the conditions of this invitation represent the tenuous situation in which I find myself. This is a meeting to prepare the company's sales team for the coming year. I was invited, but I am not being paid for my time, nor am I being paid for my travel.

From the customer's perspective, I am at this meeting to get a better sense of their industry. When a consultant is being phased out, there needs to be a reason. The apparent reason is my alleged inability to tie my message closely enough to their industry.

Ironically, my major concern over the past couple of years is that I know a little too much about this industry. The power of my message has always been that I am not from their industry; I am from the greatest sales training corporation in the world. My message has been to connect their industry to Xerox. That has been the unique niche that I have parlayed into a comfortable living. Now that message is being questioned.

Life consists of tests. I was being tested. I bellied up to the bar and sent myself to this meeting. I had no idea how important that decision was, but I figured it out rather quickly. When the meeting was over, the lesson was learned.

Thursday, December, 17th–9:30 P.M.
The meeting went well. My attendance, and my paying my own way, was very important. As I suspected, I was being tested and I think I passed the test with flying colors. The people who put on the

meeting went out of their way to stress the fact that I had chosen to come and had paid my own way.

It was not as relaxing as I had hoped, however. When I was introduced in the morning I was asked if I would speak for about 15 minutes at the end of the day about what I got out of the meeting. I was glad to oblige, thinking it would be a great opportunity to sell.

As I was taking notes from the meeting on my laptop, I also kept a PowerPoint document open. Every time I heard a good quote, or heard something I thought I could use at the end of the day, I simply wrote it right into a slide for my presentation.

At the end of the day, I walked on up, plugged my computer into their projector, and flew my slides and words across the screen. I don't want to brag, but the visual portion of my presentation was clearly better than any of the six speakers who came before me. Not bad since I made it up as the day went along!

After I ran my slides telling them what I felt was important during the day, I ran two final slides called "The Jolles Pitch." I clearly outlined my position and why I felt they needed to utilize me more. Who knows if it worked? I had a lot of people come up to me during the break to say that they would be using me next year.

Generating significant business means passing those tests. One of my best friends in the world recently interviewed with a company for a new job. After a series of interviews, a final interview was scheduled to have him meet with one last vice president. The meeting was a bust. My friend was challenged throughout by a relentless and sometimes mean-spirited individual.

My friend held his own, however, and was not shy about the experience. Later, when asked on the phone by this vice president what he thought of the interview, my friend said, "It stunk." The vice president apologized, told him the other twelve people he interviewed the same way thought it went well and said they appreciated his feedback. That's why he didn't hire them. It was a test, nothing more. He just wanted to see how my friend reacted to the test.

Never underestimate the importance of the tests that are placed before us in business and in life. My little test generated a six-figure consulting sum with the company that did the questioning. It still is one of my best customers. Oh, and they even pay my travel when I work for them.

Hard Work

What it is to work hard is a lesson that can be learned on the road, usually on a daily basis. I'm not referring to our own work that we are traveling to complete. I'm talking about a member of the travel network that all Road Warriors are a part of. I'm talking about cab-drivers. Quite simply, in my opinion, cabdrivers are the hardest-working people I have ever met in my life.

Friday, December 4th–8:30 A.M.

Sometimes I can't believe I have the nerve to complain about any-thing. I took a cab in from LaGuardia Airport this morning and had one of the nicest cab conversations I've had in a while. My cab-driver literally inspired me today.

He came to this country from Greece almost 45 years ago with the shirt on his back. A couple of years later, he saved enough money driving a cab to bring his wife over. They have three chil-dren. One is a doctor, one is a lawyer, and one is graduating from Cornell this spring.

He raised his family and paid for their education by driving a cab six days a week, 12 to 16 hours a day. He was beaming telling me the story. Every time I asked him a question, he became more animated with his answer. He was going to be retiring soon and proudly told me that his children were going to buy him a small house on a stream in upstate New York.

What an inspiration. I guess what I learned from this individual was that it's not impossible to make a living driving a cab. You'd just better be ready to work hard, take pride in what you do, and be the best you can be.

While we're on the subject of hard work, there is one last cultural lesson to be learned from cabs that I just can't resist telling you, and then we'll move on. As you no doubt have figured out by now, I have a real soft spot in my heart for cabdrivers. Well, there is a particular type of cabdriver I want you to look for, and that's the men from Ghana.

I don't know why this is so, but it seems that most large cities have an unusual number of cabdrivers who have come here from Ghana. I have never in my life seen a more dedicated group of people in my life. You won't believe this, but these men from Ghana *all* have the same dream and goal. They work day and night, send their money home, and build a house in Ghana. When their house is complete, they leave and go home. This isn't an activity with just some of the men from Ghana. If I have driven with fifty drivers from Ghana, I have heard about fifty houses.

Thursday, October 26th—4:30 P.M.
Coming out of Minneapolis and the story today is not my seminar or flight. It's my driver from Ghana. He seemed impressed when I

*recognized his accent and pegged him from Ghana. He seemed
even more surprised when I asked him about his house.*

*This guy's story was amazing. He had been in this country for
eight years. He not only built a house, he showed me pictures of
the apartment building he was also building. For eight years he
saved every penny of his money by driving morning, noon, and
night. His bed for the past eight years was a mattress he took out
from a closet and laid out in the kitchen of a house he shared with
other cabbies from Ghana.*

Abraham Lincoln once said, "My father taught me to work; he
did not teach me to love it." And the stories just keep coming . . .

Tuesday, June 3rd—5:15 P.M.

*Fighting my way out of Dallas was harder than the seminar. I left
at 4:03 to catch a 4:45 flight. It is normally a 20-25 minute drive,
but traffic was horrendous. The cabby that I had was tremendous.
I recognized that Ghana accent in an instant. I asked him about his
house, and he swelled with pride as he told me about its con-
struction. I told him I really needed to get to the airport on time,
and he went to work. We went over two medians, down emergency
lanes, cut people off left and right, and he got me to the airport
at 4:35. The good thing about Dallas's airport is that you can be
taken almost to the gate by cab. I tipped him $15. He was happy, I
was happy, and I jumped right on my flight.*

I don't mean to be offensive in my categorizing of a culture, but
I am only relating to you what I have seen, and I make my obser-
vations with respect. My driver Sam is from Ghana, and his house
is coming along fine. My hat's off to the men of Ghana! These are

inspirational people who work hard for an honest and decent goal. By the way, if called upon, they can drive a mean cab.

Hustle

Often you hear in business that the one who hustles is the one who wins. Road Warriors learn all about hustle, not just from the business they conduct, but the travel they participate in to conduct that business. If you want a classic example of this, watch your local Road Warrior come slipping onto that plane right before that door closes. Even with all the airline changes, the potential still exists for what I call "the perfect catch." The perfect catch is like the perfect race. It's getting on that plane somewhere between consciousness and unconsciousness as they shut the door . . .

> **Saturday, August 15th–8:45 A.M.**
> It's been an early one. Pickup from the hotel was 5:45 A.M. I was booked on a 7:05 A.M. flight out of Aspen. This flight was due to arrive in Denver at 7:45 A.M. My departure to Dulles was 8:12 A.M. Sounds a little scary? It gets worse.
>
> Aspen is really an amazing travel destination. All flights in and out book an average of two months in advance. Every flight is oversold and every flight has delays. I suppose we were lucky. We left at 7:30 A.M. With an estimated flying time of 30 minutes, I calculated 12 minutes to taxi, deplane, and get to my next gate.
>
> True to form, we landed at 8:01. I have to admit, I've never seen a jet taxi like this one. We got to the gate at 8:06. The guy in front of me went down the aisle before the plane even stopped, and I was right behind him. We came in at Gate 60 at Denver International. I checked the monitors to find out that my departure was out of Gate 29.

*In the thin Denver air, I ran about a half a mile. I did it in four
minutes. The flight wasn't even on the last monitor I passed. When
I got to the gate, the lights were out, but the door was open. The
United person laughed when he saw me wheezing for air, but
shook his head and said, "You earned it, climb on board." I got on,
they closed the door behind me, and away we went.*

By the way, the airlines don't refer to these scenarios as "the perfect catch." They refer to a passenger who arrives late, running and
sweaty from fighting to get to the departure gate, as an "NFR."
Now, what do you think that stands for? Give up? It stands for
"'nother friggin' runner!"

I've coached kids' basketball and soccer for more than twenty-
five years, and have had more than fifty teams. I thought I knew all
there was to know about coaching, but recently attended a coaching clinic that was put on by one of my basketball heroes, Kevin
Grevey. It was one of the best clinics I have ever attended, but the
showstopper for me was when Kevin addressed the issue of winning. He told us a story about the best coach he had ever had, Don
Nelson. He told us that in his years of being coached by Don, not
once did the coach ever say, "Go out and win." What he did tell the
team was things like "Go out and do the best you can" or "Go out
and execute what we've practiced"—but never "Go out and win!"
So, the lesson in hustling really centers on your criteria for winning. My hope is that you look at the big picture and attach your
victories to effort and desire.

CHAPTER FIVE

Danger Zones and Detours

S ometimes the road seems littered with land mines. No two days are the same, and each trip presents the Road Warrior with a unique set of obstacles. These obstacles can become danger zones, and your ability to sidestep these problems can save your neck.

Now the lessons begin to focus on the real world, which can be harsh and unforgiving. Can you regroup and come back from the setbacks that attack any Road Warrior? It starts with the simple things—ideas as easy as reading the fine print, or just asking questions and listening. What are the warning signs and landmarks that will keep you clear of danger, and that includes avoiding one of the most significant quicksands of being a Road Warrior . . . the hotel bars. Can you trust your instincts and your hunches? Finally, can you avoid the slow, insidious threat of boredom?

Reading the Fine Print

Misunderstandings can sometimes be found in the fine print, and the poster child for misunderstandings is the airline industry. Don't try to litigate your anger, because all these misunderstandings can be cleared up if you simply read the fine print. Just look at your ticket. It looks something like this:

> The party of the first part protects the party of the second part, defining the party of the third part.

Well, here's a little fine print of my own . . .

> If you can read or understand this, you are a better person than I am.

The fine print might appear trivial to you, but you never know when that fine print can ruin a deal for you. Let's use the words "Confirmed Seat" as an example. The airlines will tell you again and again that if you have a confirmed seat, you have nothing to worry about. That's just not true. If you are not sitting in that seat, you still have plenty to worry about.

Wednesday, March 17th—7:05 A.M.

This one got nasty. We're airborne almost three hours late, and believe it or not, I'm in a pretty good mood. You see, I learned a lesson in perspective.

When our plane finally came in, we were informed that the flight was oversold. Now, that's not that unusual. They offered the usual pathetic $300 in flight credit as they tried to entice seven people to give up their seats. We were all tired and frustrated. No one gave up a seat, especially for that. The big airlines start at $300, but the offer keeps going up until they have enough volunteers.

Then they just started calling names. I listened as these people were informed that they were being taken off the flight. They had two choices. They could "volunteer" and receive the $300, or they could be "mandatorily removed" and receive nothing. These were people who had confirmed tickets. Unfortunately for them, they were the last seven to confirm.

> *When they started to complain, the nasties who worked for the airline reminded them that this information is on their ticket. In fact it does state, in incredibly small print, that the airline reserves the right to take your seat if they feel it is necessary. The people removed weren't even thanked.*
>
> *So, here I sit, in a packed puddle jumper, despising the scoundrels who operate these embarrassments, happy that they let me take their rude, late, no-service airline. You see, life frequently does provide us with lessons in perspective.*

In all fairness, I must say, I've never seen an occurrence like that again, but it's kind of scary knowing what the airlines can get away with. The lesson here is, if it's important to you, don't blindly accept information that is presented to the masses. As an example, I wouldn't go by the airline monitor, but instead I would force the airline personnel to tell you exactly where the arriving flight is. If you sense trouble, move on and catch another flight. Don't apologize—just go. If the airline doesn't like it, just tell them to read the fine print:

> If you can't tell me what I need to know, I can take my business to any other damn airline I want to!

When you are about to climb into another company's culture, ask questions to uncover the basic facts, and perhaps you will avoid the misery of being the casualty of poor timing.

Asking Questions and Listening

Are there two more important weapons in business or in life than to ask questions and listen? Road Warriors move fast, but on the road you learn you'd better not move too quickly. When there's a delay, the temptation is to run. It would be good to ask, "Why is the plane delayed?" In business, we are often insulated—kept away from the people who can really answer the questions that need to be asked.

For instance, the best people to ask in travel are the pilots, but how accessible are they? When I see a pilot checking the manifest or walking to get a cup of coffee, I start moving in. I usually park myself near the side of the ticketing podium to catch any of the whisperings from airline personnel. You might be able to get a head start over other displaced passengers if that flight is canceled. You never know what you might hear . . .

Monday, November 9th—4:30 P.M.

I'm sitting on a regional carrier for a major airline, heading toward Pittsburgh to connect to my Washington flight, and boy, do I feel lucky! I escaped from Tampa, just barely, with my life.

Our flight was delayed, and ground personnel were desperately trying to get our plane off the ground. The plane wasn't exactly a puddle jumper, but it was close. It was an old twin prop airplane that looked tired and run down. We were waiting through a mechanical delay with maintenance on board working on our old bird. I hovered and heard them tell passenger after passenger that the delay wouldn't be long.

Then I witnessed something I had never seen before. The pilot came off the plane, walked up to the airline personnel, and told them the plane wasn't safe. The airline personnel were agitated and told the pilot that maintenance had everything under control. One thing led to another, and finally, the pilot in a hushed but frustrated tone said, "I don't care what you say, I'm not flying that plane!" He stormed off, and while the other passengers sleepily

read their newspapers, I took off and jumped on the next flight out
of there!

It's been said that knowledge is power. Having access to that information is a whole other question. Don't be intimidated into avoiding those who truly may know the answers to your questions based on perceived status or power. As my dad always said, "They put their pants on the same way you do—one leg at a time."

Sometimes, that knowledge and power can come from you. If you ask the questions you need to ask and listen for the answers, you might save yourself from making silly mistakes. That means making decisions based on real information and not reputation. It's been said the only time you realize you have a reputation is when you're not living up to it. Take hotels, for example. We become attracted to five-star hotels and other institutions that have a positive reputation. Sometimes, we blindly trust these reputations, and don't ask the questions we should be asking. You see, even the finest hotel chain, despite its reputation, can provide a few surprises . . .

Friday, February 26th—9:30 A.M.

Well, if this doesn't beat all! Judging by the name out front, I think I'm at my hotel. I came cruising into London today and was greeted with a real shock. I don't know whether to laugh or cry. This seemed so easy when I made my reservation. I mean, come on, I'm at a Hyatt . . . sort of.

When I climbed out of the cab, I couldn't believe I was in front of my hotel. I have never seen a Hyatt that wasn't somewhat massive, so I was expecting a good 20-story structure at least—not a tiny three-story building that looked more like a bed and breakfast than a Hyatt!

The people in the hotel saw it differently. The hotel seemed to be fiercely proud of its place in history. This Hyatt boasted of its size as a badge of honor. Signs in my tiny room announced that I was fortunate enough to be staying in "The World's Smallest Hyatt." I don't believe there were more than 20 rooms in the entire hotel. In-room dining was out and so was a pool, weight room, or any other typical Hyatt amenity. I guess all Hyatts are not created equal.

With all that I know now after visiting London, I'd stay there again. It is, however, a great example of making a decision based on reputation, and not homework.

Location, Location, Location

Location, location, location. It works for real estate selection and it isn't bad for hotel selection, either. Usually, the hotel represents a housing choice for the evening but not for the day. Why are you in town? Where do you need to go? Where is that destination in relation to your hotel? Be careful that your allegiance to a particular hotel chain doesn't get in the way of intelligent, sound hotel selection thinking . . .

Wednesday, August 15th—7:15 A.M.

Ouch! I'm hurt and I'm worried. In my blinding desire to accumulate my precious Hyatt points, I made a hotel selection mistake. Instead of staying at the hotel where the training is to be held, I am across town at the Hyatt. Instead of being able to wake up, wheel my materials right into the room, and get a cup of coffee, I had to cab it to my location, hauling my things with me. That's where the trouble began.

To become as portable as possible, last night I emptied my suit-case and filled it with books: 20 books, to be exact! I would con-servatively estimate the weight to be about 40 pounds. Attached to that suitcase is smaller case that carried 15 tape recorders with an estimated weight of about 20 pounds. In another bag, I have 35 participant guides and 15 more books with a weight of about 40 pounds. Finally, I have my LCD projector, my laptop, and an 8mm player weighing at least 40 more pounds.

When I hailed my cab to the training site, it happened. Foolishly, I went to put the first 80 pounds in the cab's trunk. It was awkward. I had to lift it lengthwise, move it away from my body and then gently put in so that it would not damage the tape recorders. Extending out and down, I felt a sharp pain in my back.

The only way to describe the pain is to say that I feel as if I have broken a rib. Right now, I can't get a deep breath without a lot of pain. If there is good news, it's the location of the pain. It is not located on my spine. It feels like it's sort of behind my shoulder blade. It hurts like hell, and the class starts in less than an hour. All this for some Hyatt points!

Any other questions as to why I remind you about location? It holds true in real estate, and is reinforced on the road. When it comes down to figuring out where to stay, the three most impor-tant criteria are location, location, location.

Hotel Bars

Oh boy, you are not going to like this one! Maybe I'm getting a lit-tle preachy here, and maybe I should dedicate this lesson to the professional speakers, but those bars are trouble. If you don't believe me, ask yourself this one question. When was the last time you were on a business trip, hit the bar for some drinks, and improved your performance the next day?

I can't come up with any lesson that has me drinking in a bar and learning anything positive. I now present you with an entry that will no doubt remind you of what happens when you listen to Mr. Booze . . .

Tuesday, September 28th–11:00 P.M.

I got to the hotel and never got past the front counter. It was my customer and he wanted to have a couple of drinks. I had a couple of drinks and didn't feel so good this morning when I woke up.

It happens. I'm not a big drinker, but I have a social drink now and then. The problem is, being a Road Warrior requires a lot more concentration than being a Suburban Warrior. A lot more things can go wrong when you are traveling than when you are at home.

That's my short safety speech. How about your business? Somebody just spent a couple of thousand dollars in travel expenses to send you somewhere to be your best. That's an awesome responsibility—to be your best.

Thursday, April 8th–5:30 P.M.

Ugh. I was never crazy about Julius Caesar and now I flat out hate the guy. Caesar is the man who helped contribute to this hangover. I landed in Montreal to give a seminar to a bunch of printers. I came in with another trainer by the name of Wade. Wade took the first day, and I took the second. I'm not sure I have team taught in ten years.

Well, Wade goes through his spiel and all seemed fine. As a matter of fact, it gave me a rare opportunity to bond with the group. Heck, I wasn't doing much, anyway. Each break, during lunch and after the class, we bonded. Wade was busy setting up, so it was just 25 Canadians and me. I was having a blast.

That evening I snuck out of my room for an emergency candy bar, and I was spotted. After a few feeble excuses, to the bar I went. I had my one beer maximum and worked at it slowly. The next thing I know the table had ordered me another one.

I wasn't happy, but figured, "What the heck." It's when the third one came that I got a little uncomfortable. This was now my one month quota, but I was in Canada, and they were awfully nice people.

Then I was asked if I had ever had a Caesar before. "What's a Caesar?" I asked. It was described as a kind of Bloody Mary with clamato juice in it. Three beers and now vodka with tomato and clam juice? No, definitely not.

Well, my Canadian friends had obviously been paying attention in the sales school we were putting on that day, because they went to work. I believe the reference to becoming a "Canadian brother" was the one that finally wore me down.

For two more hours I can honestly say I truly loved those Caesars. We sang songs, lost count of the Caesars we were drinking, and for a brief and shining few moments, the United States and Canada were one. I staggered back to my room and feel asleep to the gentle spinning of my king-size bed.

Then came the morning. I woke up around 5:30 A.M. and did not feel well at all. By 6:00 A.M. I felt much worse. My class was to start at 8:00 A.M., which left me two hours to get myself together. That was no small feat, since I was having trouble step-

ping out of my bed, let alone getting ready to speak for the next eight hours.

6:30 A.M. came and I finally willed myself out of bed. The last time I had felt this way was during my University of Maryland days, and I was merely a participant.

7:00 A.M. came and I prayed that I would be sick.

7:30 A.M. came and my prayers were answered. I looked terrible and felt worse, but at least the imminent danger was over. I was not going to hurl in front of my trainees. That little humiliation had been saved for the privacy of my room.

8:00 A.M. came, and I delivered that program. I won't pretend to tell you that it was the greatest seminar I have ever delivered, but I will say this. It was the greatest seminar I delivered with a hangover the size of Mt. Everest dogging me for eight straight hours.

That was the last time I ever drank more than one beer in a hotel bar the night before I had work to do. The temptation is always there, and the persuasion of those who will lure you to drink with them can be powerful. From a man who has been there, I leave you with this simple reminder:

If you're a person who likes the bars while on the job,
Prepare yourself now
To pray to the porcelain gods.

Instinct

How many times have you ever heard a little voice in your head cry out, "Listen to me—I know what's best here!" It sounds a whole lot like the little voice in many men's heads that often says,

"Please don't open the map, I know where we're going . . . sort of!"

Once upon a time, I used to call that voice "natural knowing," but now I simply call it "instinct." It's a voice that has to fight to be heard, because the conscious, reasoning voice seems to be a lot louder. Still, that little instinct voice loves to rub it in when it's right.

Thursday, August 3rd—4:00 P.M.

This has been a rough trip for travel, and today's little escapade was, in a word, unique. When I finished up my work, an old, ratty taxi was waiting for me to take me back to Albany. It was a 45-minute ride from Glens Falls where I was working to the Albany airport, and I only had an hour to catch my flight. Honestly, I just didn't like the looks of that cab.

When I got into the cab, I noticed the red engine light was on. I mentioned it to the driver who told me, "That's always on." Gee, I felt better—not! A little voice inside me was trying to be heard. It was saying, "Don't get in this cab."

As we passed through town, while waiting at a red light, the engine not only conked out, it didn't even turn over when my driver went to start it. The driver immediately called his dispatcher telling him, "This cab is dead!" Unfortunately, before the dispatcher even responded, he tried the engine one last time, and it grudgingly turned over and started.

We left Glens Falls and took to the highway. We had 40 miles to go. Fifteen minutes later, I thought I felt a slight bounce to the cab. I looked at the speedometer and noticed we were losing speed: 70, 65, 60, 55—the cab was now lurching. My little voice was not so little anymore.

Not so little anymore. When instinct becomes reality, that little voice seems to gloat at the top of its lungs, "I TOLD YOU SO, BUT YOU WOULDN'T LISTEN!"

35, 30, 25—pow! Something blew in the engine and we both went a little pale. We were now heading for the side of the road, and my driver was on the radio pleading for help.

20, 15, 10, 5—dead. At this point, there was so much smoke pouring out of the engine, I grabbed my laptop bag and suitcase, which had both been at my side, and hustled out of that cab. That little voice in my head told me to run away, and this time I listened. As a matter of fact, I moved up the highway about 100 feet away.

Soon my cabdriver joined me, apologizing for the mishap. He told me he didn't really want to take that cab, but his dispatcher made him. My little voice, which was completely in charge now, told me that wasn't true either, and I just walked away.

After about 15 minutes of waiting, one of the students I had been teaching saw the cabdriver, me, and my little voice looking miserable standing on the side of the highway, and pulled over. He hustled me off to the airport and I made my flight with seconds to spare.

Instinct is a funny thing. It taunts you when it's right, and it's nowhere to be found when it's wrong. So when do you listen, and when do you ignore it? If I knew the answer to that question, I suppose you would be spending a lot of money each minute dialing my pay-per-minute number to find out.

However, perhaps the credibility of instinct depends on experience and feel. For instance, the next time you have a tight connection, and a ratty old taxi pulls up with its engine light on and conks out five minutes into your trip, call another taxi. Maybe this is instinct, or maybe it's just wisdom.

Hunches

Hunches are a funny business. To me, they are similar to instinctive moves, with one tiny exception. The underlying judgment is not based on fact but rather on feeling. A hunch can be overwhelming in some regards and can lead any of us on the path to temptation . . . or at least, Las Vegas . . .

> ### Monday, September 14th–1:00 P.M.
> *I switched my flights last week from the one and only nonstop to an earlier connecting flight. I did this because my beloved Redskins are playing on Monday Night Football, and I would have missed the entire game.*
>
> *I also wanted to get there earlier to put a bet down. It's been about two years since I made a bet, and since I always take $100 for gambling when I go to Las Vegas, I figured I'd put it on my team . . . legally. One doesn't get to Vegas often, especially when one's team is playing, so this one's making a bet!*

I guess you can see it coming. Perhaps you now have a hunch that Rob Jolles is about to lose some hard-earned cash. Brilliant! Where were you when I needed you?

> ### Tuesday, September 15th–6:00 P.M.
> *This one did make a bet! The line in Washington for the game was the Redskins and 5 points. In Vegas, it was 6½. What luck. The Redskins scored a touchdown the first time they touched the ball, and I was downing my Chinese food in the room–up 13½ points. Money*

went down on the 49ers late, and I found out why. Final score: San Francisco 45, Washington 10. I got crushed. Sure glad I moved up my flight to make that bet . . . not!

Is this an appropriate lesson in life? Sure, why not? It was learned on the road. I can't say that all hunches are bad, but the moral of this story is, if you ever get a hunch, and you take that hunch to Las Vegas, and money goes down late against the team you were preparing to bet on, walk away. See? This lesson probably just paid for the cost of this book, and, uh, a few dozen more.

Battling Boredom

I remember once being told, "Bored people are boring people." At the risk of being called boring, I can comfortably say it has been over thirty years since I ever uttered the words, "I'm bored."

Being raised by a father who was a serious disciplinarian, I was given pre–Road Warrior anti-boredom training. When I was punished, I was sent to my room for long periods of time. Once, I was punished for an entire week. Other than coming out to go to school and to the bathroom, I never left my room. I even ate in my room. When I finally emerged, I had learned how to juggle.

Another time when I had been punished, I emerged as a fairly good guitar player. Once, I came out with over twenty pages of documented results from my A.P.B.A. baseball game. The Washington Senators won the World Series almost fair and square.

As a Road Warrior, frequently I am reunited with my occasional isolation training. Sometimes I write, sometimes I watch ESPN and order room service, and sometimes . . . well, let's put it this way—boredom can do strange things to people.

Friday, October 13th—6:15 P.M.

Normally, on a longer trip, I try to do something that will signify a reward for my final night. I've been on the road in Nashville for four nights and I feel like I've just got to do something different tonight. The problem is, this feeling is getting out of hand!

In retrospect, I must have looked like a squirrel collecting nuts for the winter. It started on day one, when I pocketed some candy from class for the final night. On day two, I took a large Sprite from the snack table. On day three, I got really weird.

I drove to Toys "R" Us to see if I could find something to keep me from going crazy on my final night. As unbelievable as this might sound, I ended up buying a small amount of Play Doh. On day four, preparing for my final evening, I packed some popcorn from the day's snack cart. I wanted to make my final night a fun one. I looked like Santa going through his sack of gifts.

I guess I succeeded. I ate like a pig and made some pretty interesting things out of my Play Doh. Housekeeping must still be talking about the remains found in Room 734. Ah, the life of a Road Warrior. Pretty glamorous, huh?

The road will test your ability to fend off boredom. It might be a different city and a different hotel, but those four walls all start looking the same. Life can really mirror this lesson as well. Certain daily criteria may change, but the job, the car, the home, and the personnel around us remain the same.

It all depends on how you look at things. Some days, in fact, *are* special. Some days can be manufactured to be special. It often boils down to a simple test of personal creativity and initiative. Here's hoping you're able to turn your boredom into exciting and memorable moments. If by chance you need an idea or two, just ask your local Road Warrior.

CHAPTER SIX

Battling Slumps and
Other Emotional Traps

This next section's lessons are a bit more personal. Some lessons can be a bit painful, but with pain comes growth. With growth comes learning, and with learning comes wisdom. It's been said, "When you're not growing, you're dying." I find that phrase a little dramatic, but I certainly understand its message. But did I mention that growth can be painful . . . ?

These next lessons focus on the often-clumsy search for a way out of the troughs we sometimes find ourselves in; this is all part of personal growth, and the necessary learning that is a fortunate by-product. What happens when you lose confidence, perhaps the most critical element in business for a Road Warrior? How does arrogance factor into all of this, and what specifically can be learned from what should be another honorary four-letter word, *defeat?*

Confidence

One of our most valuable treasures is confidence. Without it, whatever task we attempt is in jeopardy. For anyone who has to get up and speak for a living, confidence might very well be the most critical weapon in the arsenal. Could you imagine hearing someone like me get up and say, "I'm here to change your lives today. Unfortunately, there's just one problem. I'm not sure I currently possess the skills to be of any help."

In my fifth year in business for myself, after eleven years of public speaking, I faced the crisis of lost confidence. It didn't happen all at once. Its onset was slow and rather unspectacular. In retrospect, I suppose that's in keeping with these types of situations. Nevertheless, when this lack of confidence made its appearance known to my consciousness, it was one of the most difficult dilemmas in business that I ever faced.

> **Friday, October 2nd—3:45 P.M.**
> The seminar went OK. Once again, I really wouldn't fault my performance too much. This was a group from Bank of Oklahoma. I saw speaker after speaker before me fail miserably. I got more out of the group than all of them combined.

This was not the first entry that began this way. Part of the viciousness of a problem like this is the denial that accompanies it. Fortunately, that entry did not stop there.

> In a way, I'm in a little slump right now. Part of me wants to believe it is my audiences, but just a part of me. The other part is trying desperately to go over what I'm doing and how I'm doing it. Am I missing something? Am I displaying arrogance? I wish I had someone who could watch and give me straight, honest feedback.
> This is the real life of a Road Warrior. It is a day-to-day, city-to-city, and for me, presentation-to-presentation existence. It is fragile, and at times like these, it is a little scary. But I have a couple of things working for me.
> I have a willingness to look inside and question myself. This means climbing down off the horse and taking a hard look at me. I am human, I have flaws, and not only am I not perfect, I will never be perfect. But I won't stop challenging myself to be better, and I

will never listen to the voice in my head that wants to redirect full
blame away from me.

So what is working? One thing I have going for me is my enthu-
siasm. Even when I stumble through these somewhat disappointing
times, I always have my enthusiasm. I once called it the "great
equalizer," and I still believe it to this day. I'll get up, and I'll push
on. I will watch for arrogance or any other possible culprits. But
rest assured, I'll do this with enthusiasm.

I'm rather proud of that entry. We all struggle and we all are
challenged. What I learned is that when we face these challenges,
we have two lines of defense. First is study. Are you willing to look
inside yourself and question the source of your struggle? This is
not an instinctive behavior. As a matter of fact, I believe we are pre-
disposed to react in an opposite manner, and that predisposes us
to become the worst creature known to mankind—a professional
victim.

Sometimes it's easier to understand this creature by considering some of our friends or loved ones. How many people do you
know who always seem to have bad luck? The plumber is suing
them. The boss doesn't like them. The second wife doesn't understand them. The neighbor is mean to them. It goes on and on, with
one common theme. The people who are cruel to them seem to
act this way for no apparent reason.

Ask a professional victim, "Is there anything, *anything* you
could have done differently?" and they will tell you, "No!" I find
this to be one of the saddest afflictions that can possibly reside in
a person's soul. You see, quite simply, they are missing one of the
most critical elements that we as human beings can possess. With-

out questioning ourselves, we cannot learn. Without learning, we cannot acquire wisdom.

I am both frustrated and baffled by professional victims. I'm thinking of one I've known for many, many years. Perhaps he unwittingly taught me this lesson. His inability to question, learn, and change has subjected him to a rather ironic condition. He has spent a lifetime repeating his errors and duplicating his flaws. Can there be a sadder fate? I know of no successful person who possesses this flaw. Need I say more?

The other line of defense for a lack of confidence is optimism. It seems like a contradiction when you think about it. On one hand, I'm recommending that you never stop questioning the way you do things, yet on the other hand, I say you never stop believing in the way you do things. These two tips may seem like strange bedfellows, but together I believe they are what make it possible to harness and use confidence. They coexist because the time to self-actualize is not in the heat of the moment but rather in the aftermath. In fact, optimism did help move me through my crisis. This crisis lasted almost half a year, but my optimism never wavered. I did believe that I would eventually figure it out and work myself through it.

Wednesday, November 18th–7:30 P.M.

Was I tremendous? Debatable. Was I damn good? Not debatable. Before I blather on about myself, the true measurement for success in my business is determined by the additional business that comes from a presentation like the one I just delivered. That, I won't know for a while.

Now for a little blathering. It went well. I felt in control of that audience the entire time. They were engaged and active, asking

questions, laughing, applauding, and looking like they were hav-
ing a good time. These are some of the measurements I use. The
rest are based on "feel," and I liked the way this one felt.

After one of the longest layoffs I can remember in a long time,
it definitely wasn't perfect, but you know, I wasn't looking for per-
fection today. I was looking for Rob Jolles. I was looking for a
human being who, despite his best efforts, was struggling with his
confidence and looking for one of the most important elements a
person can possess in this occupation. I was looking for a way to
believe in myself again.

I can say this. I'm not out of the woods yet. Today was an
important step back, a building block toward repairing what has
been broken. My confidence was dismantled block by block and it
will need to be repaired block by block. I will take this success and
feed off of it during my next seminar, just as I did when I got
started five years ago. When this process is completed, I really
believe I will be better from the experience. Perhaps this is the
process one goes through to reach the next level.

I once heard it said that if a true optimist ever fell in a lake, he
would come up checking his pockets for fish. The key is to hang
on to realistic optimism, and avoid the crutch of excuses. It all con-
tributes to the validation of passing the proverbial buck.

Excuses are nothing more than the mind trying to soothe the
soul. Not that this is always bad, but the one thing that concerns
me about excuses is that they can deceive the rest of the body.
Excuses provide a convenient way to avoid learning. Without
learning, you might as well begin working on a lot of excuses.
You're going to need them.

Arrogance

Now that you've witnessed my time of grappling for answers, are you curious what my half a year of questioning finally taught me? It taught me lessons in confidence, learning, excuses, effort, and playing the victim. But one last domino was still standing tall. The hardest part was figuring out what the illness was. Once detected, the last solution was not that difficult.

I'd like to tell you that my journal entries and self-analysis finally identified a fatal flaw that was hounding me, but I cannot. As with many lessons learned in life, the most striking lessons can be learned from the flaws of others . . .

Sunday, October 11th–8:15 P.M.

I never liked the speaker I'm about to follow, and I probably never will. He's mean-spirited and nasty to his audiences. He curses a lot, which might be part of his shtick, but if that's the case, I would suggest he start finding another shtick.

One other thing I don't like about this guy is his arrogance. He's cocky and proud of it. I am going to make a conscious effort not to come off as arrogant. Having this guy here should help a great deal. One of the best teaching tools for me has always been watching someone else do something I don't like.

I'm going to be less cocky and more humble. It shouldn't be hard because the cocky part of me is merely a persona I adopt. The real me is happy and thrilled to have an audience that will listen to me. I'm ready to go. It's my time now.

After months of disappointing presentations, I stuck that one. If that presentation had been a balance beam, I would have nailed the routine and stuck my landing without as much as a minuscule hop.

For months and months, I had been trying to analyze what was going on with me and my relationship with my audiences. After years and years of hard work, I had risen to the top of my profession, and ironically, success seemed to move further and further away. Because I now had a name, in my zeal to make sure people knew about it, I alienated the people I had worked so hard to impress. I had become an arrogant person. It can happen to the best of us. What a bizarre Catch-22! We work so hard to achieve success and the confidence that goes with it. The reality is, if you aren't careful, it can be the beginning of your undoing. For me, this arrogance was not just limited to the work I was performing. It spread to my travel habits as well.

Thursday, June 15th–7:30 P.M.

Why is it that I can put 100,000 miles in the air when I travel alone, but if I bring someone with me I'm no longer a Road Warrior? I'm a Road Worrier! I won't forget this trip anytime soon.

My wife, Ronni, was with me for this one, and I found myself enjoying the role of travel expert as we left Washington for Panama City Beach, Florida. There were no direct flights down, so we connected in Atlanta. We left Washington on time, arrived in Atlanta on time, went to the gate to check our Panama City flight and it was not only on time, it was waiting to be loaded. This was a travel lay-up.

I smell an ego spinning out of control. Showing off for the wife, letting my Road Warrior travel guard down, and inviting trouble. Well, trouble took me up on my invitation.

We went into an airport gift shop right across from our gate. I bought a few magazines and lectured my wife on the fine art of air travel. When we came out of the gift shop there was already a line forming in front of our gate as the plane was loading.

I didn't realize that there were actually two planes loading right next to each other set to depart at the same time. I never had this happen to me before, but as I learned, there is always a first time for everything.

Unfortunately, while I was lecturing on how we should immediately get in line so we could get our luggage stowed, we went left instead of right. The stewardess checking tickets never noticed, and as bad luck would have it, we loaded on an extremely light flight.

At one point, another man came up to claim the seat we were sitting in, but we had possession. I told him in a rather sarcastic tone to grab another seat and have a talk with his travel agent when he got home.

Hey! Egotism and rudeness. What an attractive combination.

Finally, right before the aircraft door was shut, we heard the announcement. "Would a passenger, Jolies, please ring his call button?"

In my entire career as a Road Warrior, I have never had my name called over the P.A. system. Hearing my name made me both proud and confused. "I didn't order any special meal," I thought to myself. In a proud sort of way, I looked at my wife and told her, "I'll handle this," as I reached up for the call button.

When the stewardess came up, in a sweet tone she asked, "Are you two heading for Chicago today?"

With my last smirk of the day I answered, "No, why?"

"Because this plane is," she fired back.

Murphy's Law had struck and struck hard. Normally, the stewardess will check your ticket as you are getting on the plane. Our stewardess was almost as out-to-lunch as I was and didn't catch it. Normally, there are a couple of announcements as you are getting seated. We heard none of them.

We grabbed our things and ran off the plane as fast as we could. The stewardess was kind enough to tell us we didn't have to run too fast because the flight we should have been on had already pushed back. I supposed the Chicago flight would have already pushed back, too, if it wasn't for the Jooooleeees family.

Today, there are electronic gate readers, perhaps invented because of pathetic travelers like the "Jolies family." However, remember this. Those readers are frequently not working, and when they are, I would still recommend a couple of peeks to confirm the flight you are about to get on. Just make sure to stow your runaway ego along with your bags, and the trip will be a lot smoother. Consider these remarks from a veteran sea captain. I think you'll be surprised when you see who said them:

"When anyone asks me how I can best describe my experience in nearly forty years at sea, I merely say, 'Uneventful.'"

"In all of my experience, I have never been in any accident!"

"I have seen but one vessel in distress in all my years at sea."

"I never saw a wreck, and have never been wrecked,
nor was I ever in any predicament that threatened to
end in disaster of any sort."

Those words were written in 1907 by E. J. Smith . . . captain of
the *Titanic*. There's just no excuse for arrogance. No matter who
you are or what your position in life is, it just doesn't have to be
that way. Consider this last story about my friend Jack . . .

Saturday, May 11th—7:15 P.M.

*I delivered a presentation in Aspen, Colorado, today that I think
went just beautifully, but that's not what I'll remember from this
one. I'll remember Jack.*

*I was setting up to deliver a sales seminar for a bunch of senior
bank officials and I got to meet Jack. The company sponsoring the
event was a mutual fund company called Van Kampen Merritt. The
company has an interesting past. Seems like a couple of guys
named Bob Van Kampen and Jack Merritt started the company
some years ago. Both of these gentlemen are now worth millions
and millions of dollars.*

*As I'm putting participant books in front of seats, in comes this
rather disheveled individual. I figured he was a participant, although
I couldn't for the life of me figure out how this guy earned a ticket.
He came up and asked if he could help pass out materials. I thought
to myself, I probably can't get rid of him, I might as well use him. I
gave him some materials and said, "Be my guest."*

*Normally, before a presentation, I'm not the most talkative indi-
vidual you will ever meet. I've got a lot on my mind. This guy, however, was fairly engaging, and quite curious. What the heck, he was
helping me set up, the least I could do was talk to him.*

So we talked, and in the next ten minutes I had a wonderful conversation. He politely shook my hand, told me he enjoyed the conversation, and left. Once he walked out, a few of the Van Kampen employees came rushing up and asked, almost nervously, "Do you know who you were talking to?"

I kind of shrugged, thought to myself it could have been a maintenance worker for the hotel, but decided to keep that thought to myself.

"That's Jack Merritt!" one of them told me. "You were just talking to the president of this company."

I looked back to the door, but Jack was gone. His message, however, was not. Here was a man who may very well have been the most financially successful person I had ever met. He was neither arrogant nor was he inaccessible. He was just a happy, kind person.

Through the years, I was fortunate enough to talk with Jack Merritt on a number of occasions. Unless someone told you who he was, you would never know of his financial success. I take the teachings of Jack Merritt with me wherever I go. Whether it's an audience that has come to hear me speak, a friend who has come to spend some time, or a retail person who has come to help me, I have made a commitment to them all. I am committed to working hard in not allowing arrogance to be a part of my character.

Defeat

My conclusion to this chapter on emotional traps may end with an unexpected message—I hope you fail. That is, I hope you experience just enough disappointment and frustration to really bear down, stay humble, and keep fighting. In my Road Warrior world, Herb Cohen is the man who is guaranteed to put me in my place—and bless him for it.

Thursday, October 30th—7:00 P.M.

I'm in lovely Bermuda, getting ready for tomorrow's talk. What a gorgeous place! There are a lot of speakers, and this time, I like my slot. I'm the second speaker of the morning. The first speaker, 8:00–8:30, speaks on negotiation skills. I hope he is not a nice guy. That way I won't feel badly if I crush him . . . and I must crush him. To earn the fees I want to charge next year, there can be no doubt who is the top speaker.

The world of the Road Warrior is a brutal one, but every now and then, our traveling grinds can take us to some wonderful locations. I think Bermuda would certainly fall into that category. What a lovely place for a good, old-fashioned butt whipping . . .

Friday, October 31st—3:00 P.M.

Herb Cohen. I'm going to remember that name. I'm going to remember that name because Herb Cohen cleaned my clock today. Top speaker? Not Rob Jolles, I can assure you of that. Not today. Today I was clearly number two.

Boy, was that hard for me to say. I'm not real fond of number two. As a matter of fact, as I pored through the roughly seven hundred pages of journal entries, I don't believe I ever saw that statement a second time.

Herb Cohen. He started at 7:45 A.M. and was supposed to be done
at 8:30 A.M. He finished at 9:00 A.M. I only mention this because he
was given 45 minutes and I was given 45 minutes. He didn't take
45 minutes, he took an hour and 15 minutes! Normally, customers
don't like this failure to hit your speaking times, but this guy had
the room in the palm of his hand, and the customer loved him. In
an attempt to get back on schedule, the only thing the customer
could do was to cut me back to 30 minutes.

Almost like witnessing the various stages of dying (which, in a
way, as a performer I did), the first stage you have just witnessed is
denial.

Herb Cohen. He was the man today. It started with his credentials.
I've written a couple of books. He wrote a couple of books that
have spent months on the best-sellers list.

Ouch.

Herb Cohen. I have some powerful clients like Toyota, Xerox, and
Morgan Stanley. He has some powerful clients like Jimmy Carter
and Ronald Reagan and half of the United States government.

Ooch.

Herb Cohen. I had experience with negotiation training and helped
negotiate some pretty impressive Xerox contracts. He had experi-
ence with negotiation training and helped negotiate the release
of the Iranian hostages.

Oh, my, that's gotta hurt.

Herb Cohen. I'm funny. He is a Catskill Mountains stand-up comic. What he lacked in material—and there was some pretty good negotiation material—he made up in humor. It was nonstop and it was funny.

My goodness, he even out-funnied me!

Herb Cohen. The crowd looked almost disappointed when it was over, and appeared even more disappointed when they heard my introduction. I have seen that look before—only not directed at me. It creates a nauseating feeling. It feels as if someone is belting you in the stomach. It hurts. At times, this look knocked me off stride and depressed me. I battled on, though. My ego may have taken a shot, but my will to win never left me.

Imagine hearing an introduction for a speaker that sounds just like the speaker you have been listening to, only not as impressive. Then, imagine this guy gets up and has the nerve to *sound* just like the speaker you have been listening to. Time for just a little more denial . . .

Herb Cohen. He threw the schedule off at the seminar and couldn't have cared less. He was going to get his "routine" in. He was on a roll and the people running it didn't seem to care. When I got near the end of my presentation, I mentioned how sorry I was that I didn't have time enough to finish the presentation. The audience didn't seem that concerned, one way or the other. They had already seen "the man" today.

The next stage of defeat is acceptance. I had taken to the road, flown my Road Warrior body all the way to Bermuda, and failed . . . or had I?

Herb Cohen. So what did he teach me? He taught me that to be "the man" you'd better be prepared for days when you are not. He taught me that there are many levels to a profession, and every time you think you are near the top, there is another level to contend with and another person willing to shove it in your face. Deal with it.

When I started this book, I presented you with a statement regarding the essence of wisdom. I truly believe that wisdom cannot be achieved without defeat. It can humble us, but ironically, it can also teach us some of the greatest lessons we will ever learn.

Herb Cohen. He made me a better speaker today. I will lick my fragile speaker's wounds and live to fight another day. I'm disappointed that this may very well be the last sales talk I give this year. I wouldn't mind getting back up on the horse quickly, but instead, I'll have to wait.

Defeat can inspire us, motivate us, and provide us with a spark that few emotions can ever offer. The key is, What did you learn from it? If you can't articulate a lesson, the defeat served no purpose. Most likely, your penance will be to repeat the defeat until you do learn from it.

Herb Cohen. Perhaps I'll see him again. Maybe we'll have equal time, and maybe he will even follow me. I hope so, because I owe

him one. I tip my hat to him, but boy, would I love to face him in
the pit for a rematch. Oh, and Bermuda was nice.

One of the greatest tragedies of our lives may very well be our fear of defeat. How many times has it held you back? Ah, but when you conquered defeat, wasn't the victory that much sweeter? Don't get me wrong, I'd prefer not to make defeat a habit, but getting beaten every now and then can sometimes be just what the doctor ordered.

CHAPTER SEVEN

"Houston, We've Got a Problem"

The flight of *Apollo 13* provided a sober reminder that the problems that are always around us but beyond anticipation can test the human spirit. Lessons learned from the road are applicable to more than travel and business. The battles that are fought in transit—and on the jobs we travel to complete—teach many lessons that apply to our daily lives as well. Some of these lessons are just the sort of reminders that most of us need to improve our quality of life, and to teach valuable lessons to our children.

We start with a reality of our existence and that revolves around life's ups and downs. The road can be an interesting teacher if you stop and look at the signs all around you—and believe me, the road is full of these signs.

Presented in this chapter are critical lessons that can be applied to us all. How well can you problem solve, and when you do, are you really freeing yourself from your prison of familiarity? If you don't, it will not be a question of if you will fail but rather when you will fail. A lesson or two in preparation will help, but no matter how hard you prepare, trouble is always around the corner. Your ability to cope with this trouble will go a long way toward your survival on the road, and at home!

Problem Solving

How many times have you heard the question, "How are your problem-solving skills?" When I was in college, I heard that phrase all the time and never really knew what it meant. I grew up watching my dad work methodically on his *Washington Post* crossword puzzles each morning with a cup of coffee as moral support. I assumed that was real problem solving.

When I went for my first job interviews, I started hearing that question again. "We are looking for self-starters and problem solvers." I immediately chimed in and claimed I was proficient in both, understanding neither.

The world of the Road Warrior teaches many lessons, but perhaps none as effectively as good, old-fashioned problem solving.

Friday, July 30th–12:50 P.M.

We're airborne and heading home from a successful albeit nerve-racking presentation. My daughter Jessie and I walked the "Magnificent Mile" along Michigan Avenue, dropping in on stores, malls, and other attractions. Other than facing 100-degree heat, with a heat index of 110, it was an enjoyable day without incident.

In the morning, however, the fun ended. I got up at 6:15, took a shower, and started to get dressed for the seminar. Shoes, socks, belt, tie, shirt, cufflinks, jacket, and trouble. In twenty years of delivering seminars I have forgotten many things. Ties, sure. Razor, of course. Suit jacket, once. Belt, two or three times a year. This little missing tidbit was a new one for me. I was missing my pants!

Now before I lose all Road Warrior credibility, I need to mention that any Road Warrior worth his weight will be consolidating hangers when packing. There just isn't a male Road Warrior in this country right now who doesn't have his pants hanging on the same hanger as his suit jacket. Dark suit, dark pants—believe me, it can happen!

The color drained from my face as I checked the floor, all hangers, and my suitcase for a pair of pants that just wouldn't materialize. Here I was with my ten-year-old daughter, trying to show her how a real pro works, and instead she is confronted with a man as white as a ghost. I had trouble forming the words, "Uh, sweetie, Daddy is having a little problem right now . . . uh, Daddy is pants-less."

Once a year I travel in shorts, and this was my once a year. Murphy's Law had struck again. Knowing the expected heat in Chicago, and the fact we were going to be walking, I only had that one pair of shorts. I couldn't even put on some nice khakis. Oh, and that pair of shorts and shirt I was wearing the day before? With a 110-degree heat index signaling the hottest day of the year in Chicago, there were reminders of the gallons of sweat I had soaked these clothes in the day before. Nope, wearing those clothes from the day before was not an option.

With the meeting starting at 8:30, and my presentation starting at 8:45, I knew I was in trouble. Certainly there was no way to buy pants at a store. Nothing would be open. I had 40 books to sign, and a presentation to set up. Time was running out.

I put on my crusty shorts, left Jessie in the room, and went down to set up. A couple of the hotel banquet staff people were setting up the room, and in fairness to them, they gave me my idea. I noticed their pants and longingly commented on how I would give just about anything for a pair of pants right now. The pants I was eyeballing were black, and kind of a spandex material, but they looked awfully good to me.

In a heavy Hispanic accent, one of the workers said if I went to the front desk, I might get help. There might be a pair or two in the hotel. Up to the front desk I went. After they stopped laughing, they told me they would send a pair up to my room.

I was on a roll, adhering to one of the first rules of problem solving. I was thinking out of the box.

With the room set up, I went up to the room and sure enough, there were my black spandex hotel banquet pants waiting for me. The length looked good, as did the permanent, sewed-in crease that stood out just a little bit too far. I put them on and they fit like a glove. That was until I went to close them.

Now, I'm a guy who has had to deal with the cruelty of hair loss and other souvenirs to remind me of my age, but my waistline has always been a source of pride. I wear a 33 and in a pinch (pardon the pun), I can get down to a 32. Heck, if my life depended on it, I could probably get down to a 30 for an hour or two.

When I went to close these beauties, I would say the hook on the left was missing the hook on the right by at least five inches. These pants weren't even close. I sucked in my stomach and was able to bring the two hooks within two inches of each other. Moving the pants off my waist and up around my navel found me another inch. Keeping the pants around my navel, sucking in my stomach as if I was grabbing my last breath of air before swimming in a pool underwater, and doing a little jump, followed by a Tarzan yell, and voilà! They closed.

The second rule of problem solving is to remember that your final solution might not be the best solution, but if it's the only solution, it's a damn good solution!

Somewhat terrified of what I might see, I approached the mirror. Wow! From the front, I looked, well, pretty good. From the side, however, it was a different story. Being a distance runner in my past, and a swimmer now, I wouldn't say I was a person who had what some would call a noticeable derriere. As a matter of fact, I'm not sure in my entire life if anyone ever commented on that part of my anatomy. Quite frankly, there just isn't much there to notice. Oh, but there was now.

These pants were so tight, my butt was sticking out like I was intentionally mocking myself. Mortified, as I continued to turn in front of the mirror, I noticed the part of my stomach I had sucked in was creeping over the waistline of the pants. I had seen this look on other men whose waistlines had betrayed their clothes. I always chuckled to myself when I saw it, but I wasn't chuckling now.

No, I wasn't chuckling now because on top of everything else, my two minutes of bound torture was now taking its toll on my stomach. It was hard to tell whether my nausea was due to the crushing of my stomach or the visual appearance of myself I was now forced to endure. Personally, I think it was the latter.

Quite simply, I, Rob Jolles, was beginning to mutate into a banquet worker. Not that there's anything wrong with that mind you, but really, that wasn't my chosen profession, and I wasn't sure how my customers were going to feel.

The third rule of problem solving is to remember that the chosen solution is not always the best solution. There's no law against modifying the solution you have chosen.

Fighting off a growing sense of panic, I began to hatch a new idea. Perhaps my belt could help me out, cover the now-painful vanish-

ing pants waistline, and reestablish some order. Once I had my belt through all the loops, a new, but small problem occurred. My pants were so tight, my belt hung lifeless off the pants, almost groping for some waistline contact. I had to move the buckle to a notch it had never seen before. To keep with the order of the day, that buckle fought me all the way, but finally gave in. My waist was back, but my coloring didn't look so good.

I couldn't tell which was going to erupt first, my stomach or my waist. Worse, time was running out. I knew I would never last an hour and a half in front of my customers, so I tried a new idea. With the zipper fully up, I unlatched the top of the pants and prayed the belt would hold the rest of me in place. It did, but it was a precarious union I had forged between pants, belt, and anatomy.

One last look in the mirror and it was show time. I was now ready to deliver a seminar in front of approximately 100 customers with a waistline like Olive Oyle and my rear anatomy leaving little to the imagination. I even had the pleasure of not knowing whether my zipper would give way and even more of me would become immediately available for viewing.

On a positive note, with the one inch I found by opening the snap on the pants and leaning on my belt, at least I could breathe. When faced with the horror of the pants from hell, you look for anything positive you can find.

The final rule of problem solving is that any solution can be a fine solution, as long as you are willing to fight for it.

The seminar? Well, personally, I think it was pretty darn good. Other than the fact that I was running my hands subtly around my belt every five minutes or so to make sure nothing was, uh, showing, and other than the fact all of me really was showing, but behind black spandex, I felt pretty good about this one.

At the conclusion of the seminar, I tied my pants predicament to the message I was delivering and got a hearty laugh from the audience. I then excused myself, ran into the bathroom, and peeled my banquet pants from my body. My estimate on the mismatched waistline was accurate. Once I extracted myself from the clutches of these evil pants, I noticed a tag that read 28". I wonder how many 42-year-old men can claim they could still fit into a pair of 28" pants!

True Road Warriors might be some of the most creative and savvy problem solvers you will ever meet. It's amazing how proficient you are when your life depends on it. Sometimes this can be as simple as making do with what you have around you. What a wonderful lesson for us all as we grope with the day-to-day problem solving that makes up our lives.

Thinking Out of the Box

A close relative to problem solving is the art of thinking out of the box. This type of thinking pays dividends in business. The training ground for thinking out of the box, however, is found in Road Warrior travel. Oh, the joys of seeing a plan come together. Consider the following story . . .

Tuesday, May 16th–9:00 A.M.

I can't believe that actually worked! I'm sitting in a cab heading into Manhattan and I should be outside LaGuardia waiting for a cab. I don't know why, but there were about 100 people waiting for cabs. I have a seminar that starts in about an hour, and I just couldn't wait . . . so I didn't.

Sam had told me what to do in an emergency, and I decided this was an emergency. I took the escalator upstairs to the departure area and went outside. There were cabs dropping people off. I stood there waiting until I could make eye contact and went for it. As the cab slowed down in front of me, I started yelling.

"What's the matter with you? I tell you I'm coming in at 8:30 A.M. and you show up at 8:45 A.M. Do I need to call someone else, or can I count on you to keep the appointments you make?!"

The cabbie apologized, I jumped in, and off we went. As soon as we cleared the terminal, neither one of us had to explain. We just both started laughing.

If that story confused you a bit, let me tell you what just happened. Cabs are not allowed to pick passengers up at the terminal unless they have an appointment. If they are caught picking up passengers without waiting in the cab line, they are fined heavily. If you just walk up to a cab that is dropping passengers off, he can't help you. When I approached the cabbie at LaGuardia, I didn't want him to get fined, I just needed a lift. He knew exactly what was going on and played his role well. So you see, not only can you demonstrate your creative techniques, you can practice your acting skills as well!

Yep, there's no better proving ground for thinking out of the box than business travel. Want to see ordinary people do extraordinary things? Watch Road Warriors get their bags on board. Oh, I know, check one, carry the other, and don't worry because the airline's going to take good care of your suitcase. Oh, and I know a bridge you might be interested in.

Well, when working through cancellations, delays, and scrambling to get to your destination to conduct your work, often your success depends on just how far out of the box you can get in your thinking. Frequently, what's in that luggage is what allows the Road Warrior to have a successful trip.

Those bags aren't leaving the sight of a Road Warrior because of the tight connections that lace most trips. Often, we don't have the luxury of showing up early. Delays may allow us to barely catch a connecting flight, but the bags usually need at least twenty minutes to be offloaded, transported, and reloaded at your connection.

The casual traveler is meeting Aunt Mildred, waiting for the luggage, and then heading off to lunch. The Road Warrior is leaving the plane luggage in hand, jumping into a cab, and racing to be on time to a critical meeting. It really isn't an option, we're taking our luggage; and trust me, we're getting it on the plane.

The next question is, with the overhead bins getting more and more crowded, how do we do it? It isn't luck (usually); there is a creative process.

Friday, October 24th–2:30 P.M.

Well that's a move that would surprise a few travel watchers. I just waited five minutes in line to give up my aisle seat near the front of the plane to exchange it for a seat 20 rows back. This flight is oversold, and there was a lot of jockeying for position out in the gate area.

I had no time for it. I have a seminar that starts one and a half hours after I land, and I'm a good 25 minutes from the seminar site. I'm flying Delta, and I still haven't reached their elite status. I might not have the best seat in this plane, but my bags are with me, and I'm ready to touch and go.

Thinking out of the box? Not yet, but certainly a move a contrarian would be proud of. If the plane you are flying has thirty-one rows and the plane is full, usually the airlines will load rows 25 and higher, rows 20 and higher, and so on. If you have a choice, row 25 is a whole lot better than row 24.

The process continues. One quickly learns of the secret hiding places, such as the closets in the front of first class and behind the last row of first-class seats, but you'll have to avoid the stares of the flight attendants. The stewardesses hate for coach customers to take these closets early, because they want to make sure that the first class passengers get their bags on board, and this is their emergency area. Once their customers are taken care of, they really don't care whose bags are in there, as long they don't wrinkle the clothes hanging there.

But that's not out-of-the-box thinking, that's just being aware of your surroundings. If you have to hold onto those bags, and time is critical, sometimes you've got to do what you've got to do.

Thursday, July 27th–4:30 P.M.

Oh my. I had no choice. If there is a traveler's hell, I just took a step closer to it. I'm on the move to New York, and my bags are with me. It's how they are with me that makes me a little embarrassed.

Fighting my way out of Atlanta was complicated by storms. I'm flying Delta again, the only major airline where I have no loading clout. There have been cancellations due to storms, and this flight is not only oversold, it's packed with luggage-carrying Road Warriors. I just had no choice.

I tried everything. I tried to upgrade, and the ticket personnel actually laughed at me. I was ticketed way up front, so I tried to move my seat back a bit. I was laughed at again. There was such an anxious group of people climbing over each other at the door, I couldn't even creep up and park myself to the side. With hundreds of bags ahead of mine, I swear, I had no choice.

No first class, no club status, no ticket in the back, no way of getting my bags on board. Then I heard the call. It was a call I had heard many, many times before, only this time, it gave me an idea.

"All first class customers, parents traveling with children, and people who need a little more time getting down the Jetway, please load now."

At least I hadn't planned it in advance. I moved through the sea of Road Warriors dragging my bags, but with a definite limp. I made sure the person taking the ticket got a good look at my injured left leg.

Now, I'm sitting back feeling somewhat guilty about my transgression. We will be landing in New York a bit late. You see, it took a while to get out of Atlanta due to the number of bags that had to be removed from the plane and loaded late under the plane. I hope I never have to do that again, but I really had no choice.

That's not a confession I'm particularly proud of, but it represents reality . . . and a trip out of the box. Please remember, most of the time I am desperately trying to keep from checking $10,000 worth of electronic equipment that can be easily damaged by a careless bag handler. Still, I am pleased to say, I have only faked a limp once. There's no way I will ever fake another limp, although my shoulder does have a tendency to go out on me when I'm under stress . . .

Preparation

In business, preparation is often the key to success. No one knows that better than a Road Warrior. There's no driving home to pick up that one last thing you need, so you either prepare or you lose. Watch a Road Warrior pack, and you'll see just what I mean.

There's an old Henny Youngman joke that goes, "I checked at the airline counter and told the clerk, 'I'd like you to send this bag to Madrid, that one to Hong Kong, and the other one to L.A.'

'I couldn't do that,' the clerk said.

'Why not? You did it last month.'"

Thursday, March 18th–7:00 P.M.

I'm feeling the stress of this month a bit and it's showing itself in my forgetfulness. This trip I remembered my belt, tie, and suit. Unfortunately, I forgot my toiletry kit. This wouldn't have been a big problem if I had a car, or could walk to a store or a hotel store.

After walking the streets of Evansville looking for a 7-11, drug store, or anything, I wound up back at my hotel. I was relieved to find a vending machine in my tiny little hotel that actually sold shaving cream, razors, toothbrushes, and toothpaste. I bought them all except one item. I figured I had dumped enough into the vending machine, so I passed on the comb. Sign of the times . . .

Well, this morning I used my little green tube of shaving cream and the most peculiar little razor I ever saw. I know I won't be seeing the razor again, because I buried it with half the flesh from my face in the trash. It cut me from head to toe. I think it was the cream, which never really creamed. It just sort of "glooped" there. It felt as if I had no cream on at all.

The funny thing was, when I finished butchering my face, I think I figured out how to use the cream. The harder I tried to wash it off my face, the more it lathered up. There were no directions, and although I washed my face well before I started, it didn't seem to matter. Even now my face hurts a little bit.

Of course, you can prepare all you like; occasionally no amount of preparation can prepare you for life's little surprises . . .

Friday, June 5th–8:00 P.M.

Unbelievable! I've never seen anything like this before. I'm seriously bummed out, but at least I'm not alone. I just landed after a tough trip to Denver. I am carrying my sales board [a Velcro-covered board that assembles for training], so I had to check it. I got off the plane, and 100 of my nameless friends and I headed off to claim our luggage.

We waited, and waited, and waited. Finally, the buzzer went off, the light went on, and the belt started turning. Luggage started piling up on the belt and all appeared normal . . . except one thing. No luggage was being taken off the belt.

At first, there was the usual excited talking around the belt. Soon, the talk became quieter and quieter until there was almost silence. Finally, the belt simply stopped. I have seen this scene on a much smaller scale, as one or two people are left with a puzzled and confused look. Not today, however, because today, the entire plane had the puzzled and confused look.

Are you ready for this? The airline lost the entire flight's luggage! Fortunately, I broke out of my stunned trance and am fifth in line, with close to 100 people behind me. I'm guessing I've got about ten more minutes in line to make my claim. I can't imagine how long some of those people are going to have to wait.

In business, nothing takes the place of preparation. Perhaps that's what keeps us sane when the occasional inevitable catastrophe occurs. At least you won't be haunted by the thought, "What would have happened if I had prepared more?"

Coping With Trouble

I must confess to you that I am sometimes referred to as a perfectionist. I guess this comes from consistently trying to do the best job I can for my customers. Still, I must tell you, I bristle at the accusation. Oh, believe me, I do all I can to prepare for the work I do. I check the hotel, book the flights, send the materials, and work with the A.V. people. Suffice to say, I do all I can in advance to put on the best show possible.

Then the real world takes over. I can plan all I want, but no matter how hard you plan, things still happen.

Friday, August 13th–10:30 A.M.

You know, Equitable sure gets its money out of me. The last time I represented this company, my timing was cut short by a late start, and I had to skip around a bit. This time, my troubles were far worse.

With my presentation starting at 8:15, and breakfast starting at 7:30, I got up early, took a shower, was packed up, out of my room and setting up in the training room by 7:00 A.M. The audiovisual geniuses had a VCR set up in the back of the room, so they asked me not to use my 8mm player and just use their setup. Reluctantly, I agreed.

That was my first mistake.

After I connected my laptop to their LCD projector and hooked up my air mouse, everything checked out and I went back to the A.V. table to cue up my videotape. They had two VCRs, one for cueing and one that was patched through to the LCD. After cueing, my A.V. specialist moved it over to the other VCR.

Have I lost you yet? Stay with me here, because here comes mistake number two.

> With the room filling up with breakfast eaters, I asked the guy if he had checked it out earlier. He told me he did. I did not insist on having it play because I felt it would lose some of its surprise qualities. Always the showman. Without actually seeing it appear, I took his word for it and grabbed a cup of coffee.
>
> At 8:20 I was introduced, and I came up to the front of the room like I was shot out of a cannon. Boy, did I feel good! I gave what I thought was one of the best introductions to the presentation ever. Then came the moment of truth. I called out for the A.V. guy to play the first clip. Horror. I could hear it, but not see it. "No problem," I thought to myself. "Probably a loose cable. In one minute, it will be fixed."

This was my third and final mistake.

> During that first minute all eyes shifted back toward me, so I spoke. I told a joke and basically was poking fun at myself connecting my need to do a soft-shoe for a minute or two. Well, a minute or two began to escalate to five minutes, and then ten.
>
> The two A.V. guys were now frantically running around desperately trying to figure out the problem. Adding to my difficulties was the occasional sound from my videos coming through the loudspeakers. Still no picture.

When you are in front of a hundred people and need to stall for a minute or two, it isn't that difficult for someone who makes a living speaking to groups. When you can't move on and it goes on for longer periods of time, it becomes brutal.

Then I buckled down and began to perform. Without telling the audience, I basically taught them what I would have taught them after the first video clip had normally finished.

At 20 minutes, the Equitable person in charge interrupted me and asked if I would like to take a break. I was probably a little intense, but I said, "Absolutely not. What I would like, however, is a flip chart because I'm ready to give this group another presentation." You see, it's kind of hard giving a presentation that relies extensively on video clips when you can't see the video clips.

The crowd began to respond. One person asked, "What clips were we going to see?" I told him, "If I answer that question, I'm going to break your heart." Laughter. I then said, "Please don't worry, because I like the presentation I'm going to give you a lot more than the one you apparently aren't going to see."

Just at that moment, as if on cue, the video began to work. It had been 26 minutes. Twenty-six minutes of teaching, talking, walking, laughing, but most important, fighting and not giving up. I told the group, "Did I say the presentation I was shifting to was better than this one? Well, I was only teasing you. This is the real, great presentation!" As the first clip ran, I quietly advanced my computer presentation past the slides I had covered supporting the clip.

From there I attacked the presentation with a sense of defiance. I was still standing, damn it. Near the end, I talked about perspective and told them to look out the window, that it wouldn't offend me. My goodness, we were sitting in a beautiful room in Newport,

Rhode Island. Look what is around us and how fortunate we really are! They understood. They had lived this moment with me and there wasn't a face in the crowd with whom this message didn't register.

That presentation took place in 1998, and I still have people who come up to me from the audience that day. The message stuck with them. They saw a human being coping with trouble and simply not giving up or letting it affect him. Perhaps it reminded them of just how human they are, too.

You know, that wasn't the only thing I learned from the presentation. When coping with trouble, the tendency is to lash out at those around you—particularly those around you who have contributed to your trouble. When I looked back on that moment and on that particular journal entry, I think I was a bit surprised at what came next.

I also looked back at the two A.V. guys, bathed in sweat. They were crushed. I wanted everyone to hear my message. I told them how appreciative I was of their help. I told them if they came up apologizing for a problem they did not intend to happen, and I had the audacity to give them a hard time, I would be a hypocrite.

The last thing I told this audience was, "If you are going to talk the talk, you've got to walk the walk. We all took a journey through a presentation none of us will ever forget, and we couldn't have done it without the wonderful help from the back of this room." I bowed, and it was over.

The term human being *suggests that none of us can claim to be infallible. It's what makes us who we are. There was no mali-*

cious behavior on anyone's part. Ironically, these two A.V. guys helped deliver some of the most lasting messages I could ever hope to communicate to an audience—compassion, patience, perseverance, and, of course, courage while coping with trouble.

There is no such thing as a life without trouble. Sometimes these troubles are more than we can stand. Still, I hope that each time you are faced with trouble, you are able to weather the storm graciously. I believe that your survival builds confidence, so that each time you persevere, you are stronger and better able to conquer the next bit of trouble thrown your way. The key is to concentrate on winning—direct your thoughts on a positive outcome. If you can train yourself to focus on the positives, and—most important—learn how to *sell* yourself on those concepts, you'll take a critical step in becoming not just a person who can cope with trouble but one who is conditioned to be content.

CHAPTER EIGHT

Finding the Positives

L ife on the road, as I'm far from the first to point out, can be rough. It can test the nerve of even the most grizzled Road Warrior. Yet the road offers many hidden sources of hope if we will just look for them; we lose in business only if we give up our optimism and faith in people. In the air, on the ground, and in the work that you travel to do, the positives are all around, and they almost always boil down to the basic goodness of people everywhere.

In this series of lessons, I would like to present some more of the unique education that can be obtained from the road. What about a trait we all desire . . . kindness? Loyalty is another lesson that can be learned on the road and applied to our businesses, along with the haunting need to see past the differences in others. The road can also instruct us in a simple yet often-forgotten skill—the simple act of learning to compliment others. Finally, one of my favorite lessons of all is one we can easily spot in others but far too often ignore it in ourselves: The art of knowing when to shut up! All these lessons pay dividends when learning to find the positives.

Kindness

When you stop and think about it, we all are given various opportunities to display acts of kindness. Unfortunately these chances are fleeting and are rarely obvious until the moment has passed. I suppose kindness requires a conscious effort because the moments that most of us manage to display the trait of kindness can be few and far between.

Friday, May 16th–3:45 P.M.

I got on this flight in a real good mood. The flight is sold out, but I got on with my United Premier Executive buddies, got my luggage stowed, and am sitting pretty. Behind me, two people were double booked into the same seat. In the airline business, possession is nine-tenths of the law, and the man standing was getting frustrated. He complained bitterly to the stewardess, who took both tickets and melted away.

When she returned, she told the man standing that there was a mix-up with his travel agent. She then asked the man to come with her and they would give him a seat. He became belligerent and obnoxious. The stewardess apologized, guaranteed him a seat, and once again asked him to follow her. He did, but not without letting all of us know that he was a frequent flyer and this treatment was unfair. We collectively rolled our eyes.

About two minutes later, the stewardess came up to me, bent down and quietly informed me that I might be moving. I whispered back and told her I had a great week, I'm going home, and under no circumstances was I going to get angry. She seemed relieved.

Sure enough, a couple minutes later, with the angry whiner in tow, she came back. She told me that the other gentleman was going to be given my seat, and that I was going to have to move. She then asked for my ticket stub so she could write my new seat assignment on it. She wrote 3A. 3A is in first class. I was in 7C, which was only a few rows away. How perfect.

I thanked her and she moved on. Meanwhile, the angry guy was leaning on the wall that separated first class from coach. As I approached him, in his whiniest voice so others could hear, he bellowed, "Oh, you're going to first class? Figures!"

Don't ask me what came over me. Maybe it was the class I nailed in Baltimore. Maybe it was my experiences in Alabama. Maybe it was the Grand Hyatt and smoking a new presentation. Maybe it was the meeting with my publisher or the stretch that was taking me around town. I don't know. It just hit me all at once.

I responded to his public whine with a public, rather loud statement of my own. "Am I going to first class? No. You are. That is, you are, under one condition. You stop whining, sit down, and let us all have a little peace."

Stunned, he accepted, quietly nodding. I went back to my seat feeling good about myself and could tell that those who heard it were pleased as well.

Oh, I remember making that speech, having that whiner shut up, and settling into that seat like it was yesterday. Maybe the lesson would be a better one if it ended there, because it isn't an act of kindness if it is done with another motive in mind. I can assure you, the only motive I had was to shut that airline door, taxi out, take off, and get home. However, the story didn't end there.

About three minutes later, the stewardess came by looking somewhat shocked. She asked me what was I doing here? I told her I gave up my seat because the whiner was just going to continue to make everyone miserable, and besides, I had a great week and just wanted to go home. She asked me if I planned on celebrating and I said yes. She then asked me if I wanted white wine or red for my celebration?

Now I was a little stunned, but I figured a nice little airline bottle of white would be nice. She came back with a big bottle of Chardonnay. Passengers and crew treated me like a king all the

*way home. All for just being a kind person. What a nice way to fin-
ish a tough but rewarding week.*

But wait, there's more . . . Airlines can be kind, too.

Thursday, December 18th—6:25 P.M.

*It must be my last seminar of the year, because things out of the
ordinary are occurring. Of course, there is my flight. It is due in
late. I've been here for almost an hour, and as luck would have it,
because I am early, the flight is late. Hopefully, we won't be more
than 30 minutes delayed.*

*That's not really that much out of the ordinary, but the USAir
choir sure is! I am being serenaded by Christmas music as I sit
here waiting. I have a headache, I'm tired from a brutally long day,
but I'm loving this music. Welcome to Indiana. One is dressed as a
reindeer, another as a snowman, and at least ten more are dressed
as various Christmas ornaments. They aren't the most accom-
plished singers, but they're enthusiastic.*

*Obviously, I am a firm believer in the sanctity of enthusiasm. It
makes me think back on the five years of leading the "Swinging
Xeroids" and the CSC choir. I loved doing that and miss it. What a
nice thing to do. I never thought I would live to say this but, hooray
for USAir.*

Sometimes I worry that simple acts of kindness, like the one the
USAir choir put on display that day, are somehow diminished
because there isn't a strong reaction to the event itself. Well, if you
are listening, USAir, it does make a difference, and we are listening.
Keep up the good work, Indiana!

Kindness isn't just a message for the airlines, either. It's a message each and every one of us must remember as passengers. In business, when you see outstanding performance you recognize it. We do this for two reasons. First, it makes the person feel good. Second, it often inspires that person to continue to perform at that level.

Friday, December 15th–10:15 A.M.

Note to self, "Try not to fly out the morning of seminars I have in the afternoon." This has been a real rough one. Doesn't that just figure? It's my last one of the year. Forty-five degrees and sunny here in D.C. and warm in Atlanta indicated all systems "go." Danny had his first middle school band concert. Staying in town and flying out in the morning was a no-brainer.

I tossed and turned last night with one anxiety dream after another. All of them had the same theme–trouble getting to Atlanta. Fantasy became reality and during my second hour of delay due to an electrical problem, my four-hour time window to get to my seminar had been cut in half. When our delay moved into the third hour, we were told that flight might very well be canceled.

In 20 years, I've only missed one seminar. Would this be my second? I was now being told by United that Atlanta had a two-hour ground hold, flights were stacked up and down the coast and all flights were overbooked. My 7:00 A.M. flight would be lucky to be four hours late. My window was shrinking to nothing.

Then I noticed some flight attendants in front of a dark marquee finishing some paperwork. Truth be told, I just wanted to problem solve and continue to develop my options. However, when I walked up I was greeted with a rather strange hello.

"Sir, if you are on this flight to Atlanta, you need to take your seat immediately. The captain has informed us that the ground hold has been lifted and they are pushing back right now!"

"What flight is this?"

"This is the 5:30 A.M. flight. Sir, they have to go now!"

Then I did something I reserve the right to do once a year. I begged. I leaned real close and said, "Listen, I know you probably hear every sob story known to mankind, but I am pleading with you. I have a seminar with over 200 people waiting for me. I booked a flight that would allow me to be almost four hours early, and I'm not going to make it."

You know what the standard answer is here. "Sorry, airline policy," or "I can't do that, sir." I don't know why I had the audacity to ask this person to put me on a plane that literally hundreds of people would be trying to get on, but I asked just same. Maybe it was the defeat in my voice, but I got a far different response than I had expected.

She looked up, looked me right in the eyes, hesitated, and then typed. In twenty seconds I had a stub in my hand and was being quickly escorted to the door. Words could not express how grateful I was for what this woman did. What an incredible thing to do! I just left hundreds of people behind. It was as if I was chosen to go on.

Once she unlocked it, I found myself walking down a Jetway with the pilot and stewardess. The captain looked somewhat stunned.

"How did you do that?" he asked.

Unashamed, I answered, "I begged her."

The stories too often end right there. I got to my seminar with fifteen minutes to spare and felt pretty smug about my latest Road Warrior victory. However, I found myself thinking about the kindness of the Dulles rep who let me get here in the first place.

Monday, December 18th–11:30 A.M.

No seminar today, just a payback. I couldn't get the Dulles rep out of my mind. Why had she chosen me? There were hundreds and hundreds of people, why me?

Well, I decided it was a sign of sorts. What was written on this sign was "Recognize Kind People." How could I just receive this gift without doing something to say thank you? How often do good people do good things without anyone recognizing them?

I called the airport first thing this morning. I found out the name of the person who worked the gate and let me on the plane last Friday. I also found out that she was working today.

I jumped into the car and stopped off at a store and bought a thank-you card. I drove to the airport, parked, and found her. Fortunately, she wasn't working a flight. I walked over to her and smiled. She smiled back. I then asked her, "Do you remember me?"

She smiled and said, "Well, uh . . ."

I broke in and said, "It's not a fair question. You see many of us Road Warriors every day. I have to believe we all look alike after a while. Anyway, you did a wonderful thing last week. You let me on a flight that I had no business getting on, but you did it anyway. I just wanted to say thank you."

She seemed somewhat flustered and somewhat moved. I know I was. I gave her the card I had bought, thanked her again, and without looking back, walked away. On the card I'd written the following . . .

I wanted to say thank you. You probably don't remember me, but because of you, I was able to perform work for a customer that was very important. I was also able to make a significant amount of money. Without you, I would not have been able to do this.

Well, too often people like me fail to express our gratitude. I'm not going to make that mistake. There's a saying that goes, "Kindness begets kindness." Inside this envelope I have a gift for you. If you have a child, please use this gift to buy your child a nice Christmas gift. When your child asks where it came from, tell them, it was a reward for me because I was compassionate to a total stranger. If you have no children, or simply choose, please buy yourself something nice for the holidays.

Again, I can't thank you enough for what you did. Happy holidays.

~ A Grateful Road Warrior ~

I chose not to sign the note because I did not want her to feel uncomfortable or as if I wanted anything in return. I wanted to be anonymous. It was a great feeling simply handing her the card and walking away. Part of me really wanted to see her face when the $100 bill fell out of the card, but that wasn't part of the plan. The plan was to be kind, just like she was, with no intent of receiving anything in return. I feel like a million bucks, and like I did something really wonderful today.

I wish I had more stories like that one, but I don't. It's a two-way street, and with a book that does an awful lot of whining, I understand the difficulty of doing this, but maybe our actions could inspire those around us. Maybe we would see a bit more airline kindness if we were kinder to those who work for the airlines and were kind to us.

One of my favorite bumper sticker slogans has always been "Practice random acts of kindness." I don't profess to be a saint, just a person who occasionally practices random acts of kindness. I hope to practice more and encourage you to do the same. If it helps, and for what it's worth, that story represents one of the most satisfying and rewarding Road Warrior trips I've ever taken. As they also say, "Kindness begets kindness."

Loyalty

Every person has an Achilles heel. Mine happens to center around the issue of loyalty. I am moved when those around me display it, and I am devastated when those around me fail to live up to my expectations of loyalty.

I believe that many skills can be taught, but I'm not sure whether loyalty can be taught. You either are or you aren't. Oh, I know, we can conveniently justify our acts of disloyalty by pointing to the inappropriate behavior of the person we are about to betray; but disloyalty is disloyalty, no matter how you try to perfume it.

If the person in question "deserves" your lack of loyalty, why haven't you talked it out in a professional manner? I'm not saying I haven't changed my allegiances to individuals I have supported in the past. But these changes have taken place with a full understanding by both parties.

No. I will never justify acts of disloyalty. When you work for some of the major corporations I have, you have plenty of opportunities to test your theories regarding loyalty.

As a Road Warrior, I travel to many locations to work with hundreds of different companies. It isn't hard to see the political struggles and professional infighting. Those are facts of life in corporate America, and although I don't like it, it is a corporate fact of life. Well, it might be a corporate fact of life, but that doesn't mean I have to contribute to it . . .

Thursday, August 13th–1:00 P.M.

Thank God that's over. I feel very good about the job I did, but it was a very awkward job. There is a lot of bad blood between management and the person who brought me in to do this meeting. Everything she touches is wrong through management's eyes. I certainly have empathy for that position within a corporation. Anyway, I had the choice of kissing up to management or supporting my friend. It was an easy choice. I believe that management was not as happy with me as I would like. The audience was! I was semi-mobbed by the second day between breaks. A speaker knows when he has done the job. I did the job and did it well. I have one more of these sessions next week.

I hate to say this, but I'm going to generate those two invoices and get away from this account. My contact who brought me in will either be fired or quit within the next couple of months. This I know. I've seen it before, and it sickens me. I know that routine. Nothing my contact person does seems to be right in management's eyes, and they seem to take pleasure in pointing this out in front of as many people as possible.

So there my contact person stands, humiliated and beaten down. Well, I'm going to continue to stand by this person no matter what the professional consequences. What else is there to a relationship when there is no loyalty?

I was wrong regarding my employment time frame for the person in question. She was beaten down for another six months before she quit. I never taught for that corporation again. This wasn't a business choice; it was a choice based on loyalty.

I have a rather eclectic collection of friends in my life who possess all sorts of personality traits. We do share one common trait, however—loyalty. As I said in my journal entry, "What else is there to a relationship when there is no loyalty?"

Speaking of which, let's not forget that loyalty can be found in all kinds of places. I met Sam Quaye almost fifteen years ago. I called a taxi company right out of the phone book, and Sam showed up at my door. Our conversation was light, and the trip to the airport passed quickly. Sam gave me his card and asked me to call him next time I needed a lift.

Each time I rode with Sam, the trip got easier. Soon I was giving Sam my return itinerary so I could be picked up at the airport, as well. As strange as this sounds, when I travel, I look forward to seeing my friend Sam. We have mutual respect for each other. Sometimes I listen to him and his troubles, and sometimes he listens to my troubles and me. Usually, we just laugh.

One of the nicest traditions we have is at the end of every trip I take. When I come out of the airport and fall into Sam's cab, waiting for me is a Hall Mentho-Lyptus lozenge. For a professional speaker, there isn't anything better. It's amazing how often I think of that reward. Sometimes, I think of it when I am alone in my fourth hotel room in four nights. Sometimes, I think about it while I am giving a seminar, fighting off back pain in my seventh hour in front of a packed room. Sometimes, I think about it while I am scrambling to get on another flight after mine has been canceled and prospects of getting home appear dim. I have to admit, I think about those damn lozenges quite a bit. They symbolize my survival from another Road Warrior trip. Consider this classic tale of Road Warrior woe, and notice who comes riding in and saves the day.

Friday, March 20th—6:45 P.M.
Bad luck tonight. A depression has swept across our Continental cabin. We have been informed just as we were within 80 miles of National Airport that a jet has popped a couple of tires and is on the runway. That news was followed by more bad news. "We are in a holding pattern until we get more information." Bummer.

7:00 P.M.
More news and it isn't good. National Airport is now closed. Not only are they changing the tires that blew, but after the plane is finally removed from the runway, we're told a crew of engineers needs to inspect the runway. Ugh.

7:30 P.M.
Still circling. The storm seems to be intensifying and turbulence has picked up. This is a rough flight. Frustration has turned to fear in the cabin. There's a nasty storm below us.

8:15 P.M.
The mood just picked up. We are being diverted to Dulles airport. Thank goodness, I don't have a car waiting for me at National. We should be down on the ground soon.

8:45 P.M.
We have just landed in one of the worst storms I've ever had the displeasure to fly through. The last five minutes before we touched

down was dead silent. No one, and I mean no one, spoke. They are planning to bus people back to National but because there were numerous diversions to Dulles, the bus line was two and a half hours long. The cab line was even longer. Not for me, of course, because my driver, Sam, is waiting in our pickup spot. Good old Sam.

9:45 P.M.
I rarely if ever make an entry when I'm home, but this story needs to be finished. I practically kissed the ground when I got home, have fired up the hot tub, tucked the kids in, and feel happy to be home. With the weather the way it is, nobody else is coming in tonight through the air. I talked to a pilot in the cab line who happened to be our pilot from Cleveland. He told me they originally diverted us to Hartford, but because we had circled for so long, we were too low on fuel to make it. That's the only reason we got to land at Dulles.

I'm pretty sure Sam would not have been able to pick me up in Hartford! I'm warm, in my own home, and I'm about to do something I rarely do. I'm fixing myself a stiff drink.

It isn't cheap going to a therapist, and getting your hair cut can only happen so often. Quite selfishly, it sure is a lot easier to take to the road with Sam in my camp. The conversation is good, the friendship is appreciated, and the help is worthwhile.

The prospect of driving to the airport, leaving my car, and traveling seems preposterous to me now—not with my friend Sam. My suggestion is to find yourself a Sam of your own, and you'll be able to soften the blow of ground transportation and perhaps even your Road Warrior journey. Most cabbies will gladly enter into a relationship with you; although I can't promise they'll bring you throat lozenges.

There are certain lessons that are nice to know and others that fall into the need-to-know column. I'm probably not the first person who introduced you to the concept of loyalty but perhaps I am the first person who ever pleaded with you to make it an unwavering constant in your life.

Seeing Past the Differences

You won't just find people like Sam at your home airport—they can be behind the wheel or a desk anywhere if you're not blind to them. Sometimes differences that blind us can be gender based, regional, or even socioeconomic, and sometimes these differences can cause us to prejudge people who may be very important to our survival.

Friday, September 26th—1:30 P.M.

I've been on the road conducting so many seminars this week, I forgot to get confirmation of my actual speaking location. I knew it was in the Ft. Myers area, but that was about it. No problem, that's why we have cell phones. Right before I left Houston I called and one of the administrative people for Bank of America in Charlotte set me straight. It was a resort I've been to before called the South Sea Resort on Captiva Island.

By the time I landed in Ft. Myers and got to the South Sea Resort in Captiva, it was almost 10:00 P.M. Funny thing—the gated guard station had no record of my stay. Simple problem, I'd just buy a room and invoice it. I waved good-bye to my cab driver, who seemed somewhat bewildered that I didn't know what the hell I was doing, but took off.

When I went to check in at the reservation desk, I asked them to place me as close as possible to the location of the training in the morning. My heart sank as the reservation clerk had no record of any meeting by Bank of America, my client.

My cell phone would not work on this remote end of the island, so my first decision was to go through with getting a room, if for no other reason, I could start making calls. The problem was, who to call. The only numbers for the client that I had were office numbers in Charlotte, North Carolina. It was 11:00 P.M. now and no one was going to be in their office. I had no idea where in the state anyone lived, so information was not going to be a lot of help. Worse yet, my presentation was scheduled from 8 to 10 in the morning. That meant I had to be in the room, whatever room that was in the state of Florida, by 7:00 A.M. Shock was quickly being replaced by depression.

The only plan I had was to start calling every hotel in Sanibel, Captiva, Naples, Ft. Myers, Estero, Bonita Springs, Marco Island, and any other city I could think of that was serviced by the Ft. Myers airport where I was told to fly into.

The South Sea Resort is on 300 acres of beautiful island land, so a van is required to take you to what can sometimes be the mile or two it might be to your room. I've stayed at this resort before, and maybe it's the cynic in me, but these drivers are awfully chatty. Could that have anything to do with the tip they might be expecting!? Well, I'm usually a chatty guy, but damn it–not tonight! Besides, how in the world could an 18-year-old bellman/van driver do anything to help get me out of the predicament I was in?

"How are you sir?"

"Fine."

"Been here before?"

"Yes."

"Uh, did you enjoy your stay?"

I couldn't stand it anymore. "YES, I ENJOYED MY STAY! PROBLEM IS, I'M NOT GOING TO ENJOY THIS STAY! IF I DON'T FIND WHERE 35 BANK OF AMERICA CLIENTS ARE SOMETIME BETWEEN NOW, AND 7:00 A.M. TOMORROW, I'M GOING TO LET MY CLIENT DOWN AND LOSE A LOT OF MONEY! I'M REALLY SORRY TO BE SHORT WITH YOU, BUT I NEED TO THINK, AND I DON'T THINK THERE'S ANYTHING YOU CAN SAY OR DO TO HELP ME RIGHT NOW. SO, I'M IN ROOM 1717. COULD YOU JUST TAKE ME THERE, PLEASE!"

That did the job. My bellman/driver/buddy clammed up, and I began to think again. What do I do? Who do I call? A minute later my buddy spoke up one more time.

"Uh, pardon me sir, but did you say you were looking for a Bank of America meeting?"

"Yes."

"Well, I can't promise you it's your group, but I also do some work at another resort that's about 40 minutes from here, and, well, uh, the other day I could swear I checked in a couple of people from Bank of America."

We were beyond a needle in a haystack here. We were about one in 500 hotels, but he sure got my attention. My tone changed a bit.

"What's the name of that resort?" I asked.

"Sanibel Harbor Resort. If you would like, I can give you the number."

"Uh, well, yes, uh, please do. It, uh, gives me a place to, uh, start." Now I was fumbling for my words. Win or lose, this kid came

from nowhere and gave me a flicker of hope. I apologized for my behavior, tipped him well, and jumped on the phone the moment I got into my room.

In a word, that kid was right on the money.

In 22 years I've only missed one seminar, and that was due to a 26" snowfall no one predicted. In my business I'm paid to be there, not to try and be there. I've driven hundreds of miles, jumped on trains, planes, and automobiles, but I take a tremendous sense of pride of being there. You can count on a few things in this world, "Death, taxes, and Rob Jolles being at his expected training site!"

At 6:00 A.M. I was dressed and in line to check out of the South Sea Resort. I found out my driver/bellman/buddy/savior's name, put a $50 bill in an envelope, and was assured it would be given to him when he came to work. I put a short note in the envelope that said, "Thanks for the life lesson." A minute later I was in a cab and on my way to the correct location.

No one even needs to know the bullet I dodged, but I won't forget. For you see, on a dark, rainy night I was saved by a person I prejudged as having no value to me whatsoever. I not only dismissed him, I was downright rude in doing it. That person ended up saving my business life. I am grateful for both the business he saved me and for the lesson he taught me. This was a good trip.

And that is a lesson I will not only never forget, but I hope you won't either. We are all on a path. That path can lead us in many different directions, but that path—and the people we meet on it—are there for a reason. The driver not only saved a seminar for me, he may very well have saved one of my largest clients. I'd rather not put a dollar value on the business side of this. Suffice to say, the business lesson of not discounting or prejudging those around us may very well represent a priceless lesson in business and in life.

Complimenting Others

It's interesting to me how stingy we are with our compliments. I'm not sure why we are so frugal in our attempts to offer them to others. Are they some sort of precious commodity that will lose their appeal if we spread them around too liberally? Sometimes, it seems that we hoard them the way a coach would hoard time-outs. Let's not use them now because we might have to use them later and not have any left!

Late one night, on a redeye home, I penned this little entry . . .

Friday, February 4th–9:00 P.M.

I am starving for a little bit more from those to whom I am traveling. You see, when an audience is laughing, I know I'm getting through. When the audience is silent, it's harder to judge. Judging by the eye contact I was receiving, I think it went great, but it's a guess. Sadly, I never really get mobbed with kudos, because people seem a little embarrassed to offer their compliments. When they do, they almost always say, "You must hear this all the time." If only people knew how wonderful their words of encouragement are. Well, I will say this. Learning the hard way has made me unafraid to compliment others.

I'm not sure this lesson would have been learned without feeling the effects of a "compliment void" coming off the road. It's a lesson that applies professionally as well as personally. It is an area of weakness for me at home, but not on the road. There is no quota system, no meter, and no rules for making another person feel good. Expressing respect or admiration for another individual is simply a kind gesture that will most likely make you feel as good delivering it as the person feels receiving it.

Test it out on me, if you don't believe me. Rest assured, if we are ever to meet, and you compliment my writing, speaking appearance, the clothes I am wearing, or even the way I eat my Jell-O, your kind remarks will not be in vain. They will not fall on deaf ears. As a matter of fact, thanks in advance. Now you owe me one.

Shutting Up

To close this chapter that dwelt so much on the kindness of others, I must admit that one of the greatest favors I've received wasn't intended for me. In fact, learning when to talk and when to shut up isn't just a lesson that applies to covering a business mistake or illness—it's probably one of the most important lessons that can be learned in business whether you travel or not. Sometimes learning when to shut up can offer other benefits . . .

Tuesday, October 5th—4:00 P.M.

When I checked in I was my usual self. I pride myself in being an upbeat person, but when I travel, all bets are off. I'm alone, I'm focused, and if you happen to get in my way, I might just trip you. Travel is just not a social experience for me! So when I came up to check in at the Mandalay Bay in Las Vegas, I wasn't exactly exuding great vibes.

As a matter of fact, my vibes were unusually low. I had gotten up at 4:15 A.M. to catch a 6:30 A.M. flight to Los Angeles, which connected me to Las Vegas. I got off the flight in Las Vegas and waited the usual 30 minutes in a monstrous cab line for a ride to the hotel. I tell you this because what came next was completely unexpected.

When I schlepped my way to check in at the hotel, I was greeted with a rather mechanical "hello" that was off an octave, and forced. That was OK because my "hello" back wasn't much better. Then the woman checking me in did such a dramatic double-take, I actually looked over my shoulder to see who she was looking at. It turned out it was me, or should I say someone she thought was me.

With a real live smile, she told me that it would be her pleasure to upgrade my room. I said nothing. She then told me that she thought I'd be very happy with my room, I politely said, "thank you"—and shut up. I'm not sure who this person thought I was, but I knew there was no reason to do anything but be quiet.

When I arrived at the penthouse floor, I knew I was in for a treat. I was only in that room for one night, but it took me almost that long to explore the room: 2,600 square feet in size, four plasma televisions, a bar, kitchen, pool table, and too many other accoutrements to mention.

When I checked out in the morning, another person eagerly asked if I liked my room, and I said, "Sure, of course, who has the time to stay in their room when in Las Vegas?!" She smiled, nodded, and comped the room, and quietly said, "Thank you for staying with us, Mr. Tucci . . . I mean Jolles."

At least the riddle was solved. I guess everyone is this world looks like someone else. Sometimes these people are famous. It doesn't happen often, but occasionally I'll be stopped in an airport

*and asked if I am actor Stanley Tucci. With no disrespect for Mr.
Tucci, I'm flattered, to say the least. In those situations I always
say, "No, but thank you. I think Mr. Tucci is a wonderful actor." At
the Mandalay Bay my answer was a little different. I smiled, nodded, and slipped out of that hotel without saying a word.*

One of my favorite shows on television is *The Apprentice*. There
are some amazing lessons in business and life that can be learned
on that show, but in my opinion the most obvious lesson, one that
plays out week after week, is the lesson I'm outlining here. The
boardroom is where the real action takes place, and all too often
you will see promising young people talk themselves right off the
show. So speak when you need to speak, shut up when you need
to shut up, and you'll not only be more successful in business,
you'll do yourself a big favor in avoiding the words Mr. Trump has
now made famous: "You're fired!"

I've never met Mr. Tucci, but I've met my share of celebrities on
the road. I have respected the privacy of all kinds of celebrities from
my favorite Redskin quarterback, Joe Theismann—which took a
lot of discipline—to numerous actors, actresses, politicians, musi-
cians, stars, and even the Dalai Lama.

Who was my favorite celebrity on a flight? Hands down, it was
the comedian Sinbad. Not only did Sinbad gut it out with the Road
Warriors and take a redeye back from Los Angeles with us; but
while waiting for luggage, he had about twenty people in stitches
as he rattled off joke after joke. How many of you can be funny
after little or no sleep at 5:30 in the morning?

CHAPTER NINE

Victory Over Self

Have you ever stopped for a second and looked at your existing body of work? When I say "body of work," I'm referring to the collection of events that make up the moments you are most proud of. After all, isn't life really just a series of victories and losses that become our own personal résumé? Well, being a Road Warrior certainly has its challenges, but it also allows some simple, well-needed victories.

Some of these victories can be small, and others can be more significant, but the lessons all pay personal dividends. These lessons can be as simple as learning the value of an apology, or the thrill of perseverance. Finally, when examining our exploration in bettering ourselves, we must look at one of the most common elements that either hold us back or allow us to soar. I'm referring to the wonderful lessons in the decency of compassion.

Apology

Two of the hardest words in the English language seem to be "I'm sorry." I wonder why. It's amazing how powerful an apology can be. In a sense, a sincere apology is almost like a "Get out of jail free" card. It can't be relied upon if you overuse it, but boy, can it come in handy.

Thursday, July 18th–10:25 P.M.

The trip to Austin went pretty well. I did have one problem, however. I was about ten minutes into my presentation when someone came in late and sat dead center in the front row. Normally, I don't even comment. I have empathy for the people who come in late and have no intention of adding to their embarrassment. On the other hand, I don't expect to get a hard time from the person coming in late, either. I've said it before, and I'll say it again. You don't mess with a professional speaker. This guy did, and I drilled him. When I'm moving fast and focused, I am not to be messed with. When it becomes a contest, I'm going to win.

This gentleman made the mistake of mumbling something to the person he was sitting next to, and both of them laughed. I've got a hundred people behind them watching, so I innocently asked if he was settled yet, because I might need him to assist me later on. He shot back with something aggressive like, "You'd better not count on too much." I said, "Good, then I will only use you to fill my water glass when it gets low!" The whole group laughed hard at him, and I felt terrible. It all happened so fast. I thought he might mellow during the hour-and-a-half, but he did not. He looked angry and hurt.

The reason I question the traditionally conservative use of an apology is the pain we subject ourselves to by avoiding it. A flight delay would be so much more palatable if someone who was in charge looked the least bit sorry.

Everyone makes mistakes. The quality companies—and quality people for that matter—fix them as quickly as possible. This does not excuse the mistakes made, because some people are going to let you hear about it, anyway. It comes with the "I'm sorry" territory, but doesn't justify the lack of an apology.

Two major mistakes often crop up when an apology is in order. The first mistake is to ignore the situation altogether. Not dealing with a mistake does not make it go away. Instead, it allows the anger to fester and grow. I'm never happy during an airline delay. An hour later, with no remorse from the airline, I'm a lot angrier than unhappy.

This second mistake involves the words "I'm sorry." I don't mean to be contradicting myself here, but let me explain. If it's a personal relationship, and it comes from the heart, you have my permission to say "I'm sorry" to your heart's desire . . . as long as you truly are sorry.

However, in the world of the Road Warrior, we don't have personal relationships with those who are around us. Often, saying the words "I'm sorry" is the equivalent of waving a red cloth in front of a bull. It only makes things worse. "I'm sorry" has a hollow ring to it in business, and usually only makes people angrier. I've often wanted to ask, "Did you break the plane?" "Are you responsible for the thunderstorm that is sitting over the runway?"

I can remember as a kid, my older brother Richard coming into my room and aimlessly fidgeting with things that did not belong to him. I would plead with him to "put that down" or "leave that alone" but the groping would continue. Eventually, something would fall or break. These occurrences would always be followed with a monotone, "Sorry."

In a nutshell, that's the potential problem with "I'm sorry" in the world of the Road Warrior. Symbolically, this is the same monotone "sorry" we hear, and we don't like it. It is empty and useless. We don't want the hotel clerk to be sorry. We want that clerk to be empathetic and feel our frustration. We want to be listened to and acknowledged.

Well, it took me a couple of hours, but I didn't forget my seminar friend.

Then I did something at the end of the seminar I have never done before. It came to me with a couple of minutes to go. I apologized. I got a small seminar gift from my bag, and said that even the pros can step out of bounds from time to time, and I said I was sorry. It was a gamble, but it paid off. He immediately smiled, got an ovation, and seemed genuinely touched. After the seminar, he came up and thanked me. It felt so good, I apologized again, we shook hands, and it was over.

That particular trip reminded me that it's OK to bypass your ego and be sorry . . . in public. I apologized to this person because I *was* personally responsible for the problems we were having. It's really that simple. If the problems are a direct result of something you personally did, apologizing works just fine. If the problems are not a direct result of something you personally did, try replacing an apology with empathy.

Perseverance

I'm willing to bet that three-quarters of the people who read this book have had dreams of writing a book themselves. Are you one of those people? I'm going to let you in on a little secret. The secret to writing, and even more to getting published, is not as difficult as you would imagine. The secret is perseverance.

When I wrote my first book, *How to Run Seminars and Workshops,* I literally went by the book. It was 1991, and a friend of mine gave me a book by Robert Mager called *How to Write a Book.* When I reached Chapter 11, "Getting It Published," I did exactly what Mr. Mager instructed me to do. I sent out three proposals crafted precisely as instructed. Six days later, I had two offers. I settled on John Wiley & Sons, and the rest is history. Pretty easy, huh?

In 1994, I went to work on what I believed would be my greatest masterpiece. I'm not saying the world of seminars isn't fascinating, I'm just saying this. No one had ever told the story of how one of the greatest sales training corporations, Xerox, had ever taught its field force and customers to sell. I would.

With my first book quadrupling expected sales, everything was in place to beat the publishers off with a stick. With a completed manuscript under my arm, I went to John Wiley & Sons to strike my big deal. The meeting lasted thirty seconds. "There's a glut of sales books in the marketplace. We aren't interested."

Somewhat shocked, a bit humiliated and embarrassed, I moved on. I went back to my Mager book and prepared my three proposals. Three more rejections. It began to dawn on me that I might not be beating publishers off with a stick. Proposal after proposal went out the door, and rejection after rejection came sailing back. Some rejections were kind, others were not.

Weeks began to turn to months, and all I had to show for my efforts was a file with every rejection mocking my every move. Soon I had two files—one with my rejections from publishers, and the other with my rejections from agents. "There's a glut of sales books in the marketplace. We aren't interested."

I sent out so many proposals for so long that after a year, I began to enjoy the rewards of being rejected twice as I began to circulate my proposal to many of the publishers who had already rejected my work months ago. The mantra was repeated, "There's a glut of sales books in the marketplace. We aren't interested."

Seventeen months of being popped in the mouth, and I was still fighting, although I did have my down days. I mean, let's face it, what's more pathetic than a sales trainer who can't sell his own book? Then came the call . . .

Wednesday, November 6th—7:10 A.M.

I'm on my way to New York and I am, uh, anxious. A seminar wouldn't bother me. This is bigger. Today I take what I have learned in selling and apply it to selling my book. I have been invited to New York by the Free Press. They have read my book and they like it! Now, they have to like me.

I'm prepared. I have a letter from Toyota saying they'll buy books. I have a letter from Xerox saying they'll support it. I even have a tape of me doing a TV interview . . . just in case. I'm ready. Let's go do it.

I'll never forget that little Road Warrior trip. I was not really familiar with the Free Press, but I knew one thing, I was going in to make this thing work. I was calm enough until I got to the building. You see, when I looked up at the address I had been given, all I saw was a sign saying "Simon & Schuster." In my best, stumbling New York tourist impersonation, I bumbled my way into the security person. When I told him I was trying to find the Free Press, he had to hold back his laughter when he told me that the Free Press *was* Simon & Schuster. My blood pressure shot up as I approached the elevator . . .

2:00 P.M.

Wow, I don't think that could have gone better! I'm sitting on a United flight back to D.C. and I feel extremely emotional right now. Everything worked out perfectly. At one point in the interview, I was asked about potential support by some big-name customers.

I handed over letter number one from Toyota. Ten minutes later, I was asked about potential support from Xerox, and I handed over letter number two. Fifteen minutes later, I was asked about experience doing interviews and out came the video I brought with me. What a coincidence—or was it?

I circled each element I wanted them to ask for and moved them toward each of my strengths. I feel blessed to have the education I have in selling. Ever since I left Xerox, it has been my business savior. Xerox may be a difficult client, but make no mistake about it, they did teach me well.

When I got into the elevator to leave (alone), my eyes teared up. I was raised by a Marine who taught my brothers and me that men don't cry. I was able to hold off the urge to bawl like a baby, but was unable to stop the two or three tears that were streaking down my face. It has been a long, hard fight, and a long time since I've cried. I feel blessed and lucky once again. Now, in the plane, I'm shaking and feel that if I'm not careful, I'm going to cry again. It wouldn't be that terrible, except that the people next to me on this plane might not know what to make of it.

At the risk of sounding weak, I must tell you that reading that entry brings up a great deal of emotion within me. I'm not sure I will ever be able to communicate the feelings I had that day, but a lot of what I was feeling centered on the rewards of perseverance.

My desk dictionary defines perseverance this way: "To persist in a state, or enterprise, or undertaking in spite of counter influences, opposition, or discouragement." No matter what the odds are—the undertaking, the opposition, or the discouragement—fight the good fight and persevere; you may not win if you do, but you'll surely lose if you don't.

Compassion

Now here's a lesson no life should be without, so let's examine the idea of compassion for a moment. Compassion is not just sympathizing with another's distress; it's having a desire to alleviate that distress, as well.

My ethically challenged colleague wins the award for appearing in the most entries from my journals. Sadly, none of these entries are positive ones. Isn't it strange that he should appear here?

Thursday, October 1st—9:05 A.M.

I'm flying out to San Francisco, but I can't get an e-mail I received earlier out of my head. There has been a rather predictable development with my old friend. At Xerox, he was so embedded in the company, with 26 years of tenure, it took years to remove him. His cruelty and horrible business manner was quickly found out by his new company. I received an e-mail yesterday from him saying they were doing away with his job. I heard from another source inside the company that he was being fired. In any case, he sent me his résumé and asked if I could "put in a good word" with my clients.

This is the man who told me I was charging too much, was not worth it, and would be out of business in a year. This is the man who lied and cheated on work we agreed to do. This is the man who threatened to find another trainer if I didn't settle for less than an hour's consulting wage to conduct a three-day class. This is the man I sent an e-mail because he would not return my calls. My reaction was anger, but it was only my first reaction.

When we have been wronged in life, it is easy to savor our revenge. I'm certainly no saint, and I won't pretend it wasn't on my mind, but something was wrong. I began to ask myself, were his actions from the past malicious or misguided? I settled on the latter.

> I told him how sorry I was. I told him to drop by some résumés and I would certainly talk with people I knew. I told him to pick a time, and I would take him to lunch to catch up. We won't actually catch up, though. I'm going to take him to lunch and tell him what a wonderful person he is, and get him to believe in himself again.
>
> The résumés will never actually leave my office, because if he is hired, eventually my client will be upset with me. Despite the scars he has placed on my back, is this a reason not to display compassion? No matter how I phrase it, won't my lack of compassion really be vengeful, cruel, retaliation in disguise? Won't that, in fact, make me more like him? I'm at peace with my decision.

I'm also proud of my decision. He found a new job and rather quickly promised me consulting work that he never delivered. I'd help him again, though. You see, when you act with compassion, the ultimate results shouldn't be the motivating factor. The motivating factor should be alleviating another human being's pain and distress. I can assure you, for doing that, you will be a far richer person.

As with anything else, it really isn't what is said but how it is said. I've witnessed the ridiculous scenes in the airport with Road Warriors popping off to get people to bend the rules for them. However, airport personnel are paid to work with the public. It's OK to be firm, be strong, but *care*.

Second, if it's a rule, stick to it. I've been on far too many flights where the door is closed—and then reopened to let more passengers on. Much as in parenting, consistency is one of the best tools for managing difficult situations.

The airlines have not cornered the market on lessons in compassion. When you get in your cab, you frequently see someone who doesn't speak English very well. I surely hope you look a little deeper, because if you do, you will have a lot more compassion for our friends the cabdrivers.

There is a reason why your cabdriver doesn't speak English very well. For many newcomers to our land, it's the only job they can get. The taxi companies know this, and they are borderline abusive to their workers.

If you don't believe these people are being abused, look at the great deal they get from driving you in their cab. To begin with, the cab is usually not theirs; it belongs to the taxi company. How's this for a bargain? For the pleasure of driving you around in that cab, the cabdriver pays the taxi company approximately $110 dollars . . . a day. Oh, and this doesn't include their insurance for the cab. If they have an accident, they have to pay for the repairs!

Perhaps that doesn't sound like a lot of money to you, but just how much do you think this cabdriver is bringing in for a typical day's work? Well, if it involves picking you up from a major airport, probably a whole less than you think.

Tuesday, October 21st–4:15 P.M.

Amazing. I landed in New York, and jumped into a cab today. The cabbie looked pretty happy to see me . . . which I'm not exactly accustomed to in New York. Anyway, as we were making conversation, I was curious as to just how long he had been waiting. How does almost four hours sound? What a tough job.

Cabs don't just appear in front of the airport, they are waiting, and waiting, and waiting in another lot near the airport. These waiting areas are called "cab lines" and these lines can be excruciatingly long.

6:30 P.M.

I took the first flight out of Washington this morning, which got me into Houston at 8:45 A.M. When my cab pulled up in line to pick me up, I jumped in, made some small idle chatter, and then asked if I was his first fare of the day.

"Yes sir," he replied.

I then asked him how long he had waited in the cab line.

He replied, "Since 11:30 last night."

I was sure glad we weren't going around the block, and were heading to the city, which was a good $50 fare. Still, I'm always amazed at what a difficult life these hardworking people live.

The next time you come off a plane and jump into a cab, ask them, "How long was your wait?" It isn't uncommon to hear a cabdriver tell you that the wait has been two to three hours—or maybe ten! The average fare from the airport is about $25 and can take another hour round trip for the cabdriver. That means that after about twelve hours of work, the cabdriver has finished paying for his cab for the day and can *begin* to try and feed his family.

If cabbies are able, they can buy their own car, have it painted to accommodate the appropriate cab colors, and save on the daily expenses. Of course, insurance is astronomical, and the wear and tear on a car being driven a hundred thousand miles a year cuts into their profits dramatically. Finally, because the miles pile on so quickly, cabs don't last long, and the cabdriver winds up with a never-ending high car note.

This is why I have more empathy for cabdrivers than any other member of the Road Warrior's travel supply chain. It's too easy to pass this injustice off and say, "Well, these people should just find other work." That's not fair, and it's also not accurate.

You see, McDonald's might pay them more for an eight-hour day, but cabdrivers don't work eight-hour days. They work sixteen- and twenty-hour days. They also work at least six days a week.

So that prospect of a $60 fare sounds good. Then when it's finally his turn, you jump in the cab and tell him you want to go to an airport hotel. Now he's looking at a $6 fare and a trip back in line for the next couple of hours.

Thursday, March 6th–10:45 P.M.

It was late, I was tired, and I just couldn't wait for another hotel courtesy bus. I would have taken a cab right off the bat, but I know the cab routine. These guys sometimes wait for hours for their turn in line for a pickup. It is pretty crummy when that wait nets them a two-mile ride. Still, after waiting, I was cold, wet, and tired. In my best apologetic voice, I grabbed a cab. We zipped off to the hotel, but not before the guy started to complain. The cab driver behind him got out and started to chew my driver out. My driver yelled back and my worst fears were realized. I actually yelled at both of them, told the driver to get in and drive–and away we went. He calmed down when I told him I would take good care of him. Although part of me didn't

want to give this guy an extra penny, I gave him a $10 tip on a
$7 fare.

Now, before you think of me as a hypocrite and weak, let me explain a couple more things. In most of the larger airports, cabdrivers who tell the on-site airport dispatcher of their short fare do get taken care of. Normally, they are given a stamped card that will allow them to bypass the cab line and go straight back to the terminal. That takes care of the "hypocrite" charge.

As for my own accusation of being weak for tipping a cabdriver who was rude, I go back to what I said before. These people are scrapping for every penny they can. It would be convenient to punish the cabdriver for his indiscretions, but he had a right to complain. Hubert Humphrey once said, "Compassion is not weakness, and concern for the unfortunate is not socialism."

What I'm suggesting might not sit well with a customer who is paying your expenses, so be prepared to take some of this tip money out of your pocket. You won't get reimbursed for these few dollars, but you'll feel better about helping a deserving soul.

I've got one last story for you before moving on. I think it's clear that the lessons in compassion are very important to me. As a matter of fact, they may center on some of the most important lessons I've learned in over two decades on the road.

August 11th–7:15 P.M.

It has been an interesting couple of days, but the story on this trip so far has to be the hotel I was staying at. In my almost 20 years of travel, it may very well have been the worst hotel I've ever stayed at. I was so frustrated I actually took notes. Here's what I wrote during my two-day stay:

When I arrived at my room, I went to fix a cup of coffee for myself. It was then that I noticed that the coffee grounds were still in the top portion of the coffee maker as was half a pot of cold coffee. I really wanted a cup of coffee, so I cleaned everything up, and fixed myself a cup.

I ordered Chinese food delivery for dinner later that evening. I did a pretty good job of finishing it, but Chinese food always comes in a sauce. This was a sesame sauce to be exact. I got to know that sauce pretty well because when I finished my meal, I put the remains, which included a saturated bag and a couple of containers, in one of the two garbage cans in my room. By morning, it made itself known. When I returned at the end of the day after teaching, it really made itself known. It was never thrown out by the cleaning person. Nothing like 24-hour-old sesame sauce to challenge the old palate!

When I went to make coffee, once again the grounds were in the top, and the pot was half full of old coffee. The good news was, although it might not have been very sanitary, at least it was my old coffee.

Both days I was in this room some items that were used would be replaced, but not others. What was replaced seemed totally random. That went for the garbage cans too. Some would be cleaned, and others would not.

Now, here's the weird part of this whole tale. I'll bet you're wondering just how blistering my comments were to the hotel manager. Well, I wrote nothing.

As I walked out of my room to check out, I passed by the person I believe was responsible for cleaning my room. She didn't have horns, and she didn't appear evil. She looked tired, and she looked sad. I began to think, what do I know of this woman? What if she was having a bad week? What if she was recovering from a personal tragedy of some sort? What if she was so poor she couldn't dream of giving her family the things I'm able to give mine?

If I wrote a letter to Marriott, I have little doubt she would be fired. Corporate Marriott would not ask the questions I was posing, nor would they care. They would do what they are supposed to do, and that would be to fire this person. With health violations like these, there would be no warnings.

No, I'm glad I saw her because it forced me to think a little harder and it forced me to put a face to what I would have done. It was coffee in a pot and garbage that wasn't taken out. It was not a malicious crime against humanity. I've seen ruthless, mean people in business—people whose crimes were far worse—rewarded for their horrible behavior. This was not a ruthless, mean person but rather a person who was struggling with life. If she doesn't straighten out, someone else will take her out, but it won't be me.

Have I ever written a letter to complain about service? Of course . . . but not that day. In a perfect world, I think we should all be forced to see the complete picture of who it is we are potentially firing. Maybe the person I wrote about deserved to be fired, and maybe she didn't. Who am I to decide? If there was a letter to be written it should have read like this:

I think you need to keep an eye on your work. The room was not taken care of like it should have been. However, thank you for teaching me a lesson in compassion I will carry with me for the rest of my life.

CHAPTER TEN

The Way of Technology

Before you have too hearty a laugh on my behalf, I just wish I were a fly on the wall when you first handled your first cell phone. I swear this is a *very* old entry.

Tuesday, August 6th–6:30 P.M.

Good seminar, but embarrassing situation today. My phone went off in my seminar. That wasn't the really embarrassing part of this story. It's my first phone and I've had it for three months. I bought a charging cradle thing with it and put it in there every night. I thought that's all I needed to know. I not only have never turned it off, I had no idea that the phone even came with that feature. After all, I can't turn the phone on the wall at home off! I just buried it in an undershirt during seminars. The group I was talking to got a good laugh today when I explained my situation and one of the students came up and showed me how to turn it on and off. I know it's the Xeroid in me speaking, but couldn't they have put an "On/Off" switch on it?

One of the goals of writing this book was to provide as much information as possible to you the reader. Part of this information involves the actual technology that is available to those who travel. It's constantly evolving, and ultimately changing the role of the Road Warrior. Ironically, quite often for every advantage that new technology provides, something of equal importance is lost.

The lessons found in this chapter are dedicated to the technology that has worked its way into the Way of the Road Warrior. How will you end up using (or misusing) your cell phone or its cousin, the BlackBerry? What will you focus on when looking to make a laptop a part of your travels? Finally, how can you use the Web as a resource to gain information—and avoid silly travel mistakes?

Cell Phone

Ah, the blessing and the curse of the cell phone. How did we ever live without it? Oh, and how do we continue to live with it? Like it or not, the cell phone has weaseled its way into our lives. It is now a major contributor to traffic accidents, and it's creating some bizarre Road Warrior moments.

Tuesday, March 13th—9:15 P.M.

I don't know whether I'm in a Fellini film, a Hitchcock film, or a Twilight Zone episode. I got out of the cab and almost killed myself tripping over some guy who was dragging his roller board bag in front of me and stopped abruptly. Seems he didn't like whatever he was hearing on his cell phone and had to stop to collect himself so he could yell at whoever he was talking to.

No sooner did I dodge that bozo when another person came walking up to me talking to his neck. Obviously I didn't see the boom mike dangling from his ear. He truly looked like a mentally unstable person conversing with an imaginary friend that looked to me like his friend the shoulder.

A car drove by with someone on his phone. Two women walked by, each talking on her own phone. I can only assume they weren't talking to each other. Everywhere I seemed to look I saw someone babbling into a cell phone. It was creepy.

I suppose I became sensitized to the situation, but I never really noticed how many Road Warriors are fiddling with their cell phones. I was waiting for Rod Serling to appear from behind a curtain and say, "Submitted for your approval—Rob Jolles—professional speaker—Road Warrior. Tonight he embarks on a journey through a sea of people who communicate to no one but themselves. There's a signpost up ahead. Your next stop is . . . the Twilight Zone."

I don't want to sound too "old school" here, but there was a time when Road Warriors took to the road without cell phones. That downtime allowed people like me to focus. I've always been proud of the fact that despite the massive amounts of time it takes to write books, I've never written a page at home. The airports, airplanes, and hotels have been my safe haven to concentrate and work. We've lost that now, and with it, we've lost a bit of innocence. Oh, I know there's still that small amount of time when we are actually in the air, but the moment those tires hit the ground, that silence is broken.

Tuesday, August 9th—5:15 P.M.

It's like watching a symphony—a sad, depressing symphony. If there were 150 people on my flight, 100 of them were on their frickin cell phones before we took off. Some sat and talked, and some of the real knuckleheads actually came down the aisle and loaded while on the phone. Of course they whacked a dozen people with their bags as they thoughtlessly came down the aisle.

The really sad part was listening to 100 cell phones sing their opening songs ten seconds after we landed. Yuck! If it were up to me, I'd ban the damn things and create cell phone areas in airports that looked a lot like smoking rooms. There these people could cram into small areas and insensitively shout over each other to complete their precious messages.

It's truly amazing how the cell phone has crept in and taken over our lives. Everyone has one and everyone who has one seems to be on one. I think back to the days, not that long ago while I was working for Xerox, when we were able to control the communications of our students. Through the 1970s and 1980s the Xerox Training Center was the perfect training destination resort. It stood on more than two thousand acres in Leesburg, Virginia, along the Potomac river, slept more than a thousand people, and had amazing dining facilities, bars, gyms, you name it.

However, the part I liked best about it was the phone situation. All the pay phones were ripped out of the facility. The dorm rooms had phones, but these phones had timers. Believe it or not, each student was allowed a *total* of ten minutes a week. Once you used up that time, you were out of communication with family, friends, and clients.

Students were taught to tell their clients that they were going away to training to learn how to do their jobs more effectively. As a result, they would not be conducting any business while they were away . . . and Xerox made sure of it! It was a culture shock for students coming in, and they were not happy about it, but they adapted quickly. I would venture to guess that 95 percent of those students would tell you today how meaningful it was to truly get away and focus.

This is not to say that technology is always a bad thing. When the cell phone isn't misused it can be a lifesaver. I suppose you want a quick story of the cell phone coming to the rescue of your friendly local Road Warrior stuck on the road somewhere, but if I'm choosing a story to sing the praises of the cell phone, I'll pick this one . . .

Sunday, November 14th–9:15 P.M.

Jessie and I watched our favorite show together tonight. Well, maybe not exactly "together" but we were close. I'm not big on traveling on Sunday nights, but that doesn't mean all my clients agree. I do my best to move them off Sunday travel for their people, but that doesn't always work–particularly when I'm the only one traveling. This seminar was in Chicago, and the entire audience lived in or around the city. Rob was traveling on Sunday.

So, at 8:00 P.M., I got out my trusty cell phone and we talked. At the first commercial, we talked about what had happened so far in our show. We did that at every commercial and spent a few minutes at the end of the show. It would have been nicer to be together, but there was uniqueness to the experience that we both seemed to enjoy. I don't want to make a habit of this, but my daughter and I had a nice evening together . . . 600 miles apart.

And sometimes those ridiculous features that are found on these phones can become priceless.

July 15th–4:15 P.M.

Today was a special day for our family. We met as a family in Washington, D.C., and took my dad to the World War II Memorial. My father had been a part of the invading forces on D-Day and had never seen it.

*My parents flew into town from Florida, and we took them both
downtown. Among three siblings, four nieces and nephews, two
brothers-in-law, and a sister-in-law, we seemed to have thought of
everything but a camera. Don't ask how we could have forgotten
one, we just did!*

*It was then I was reminded that my phone had a camera fea-
ture to it. I snapped a picture on the spot, and we moved on. I later
mailed it to myself, fixed it up a bit, and produced copies for all my
siblings. Like the MasterCard commercial slogan: "A picture of your
hero, your Dad standing next to the D-Day plaque, symbolizing a
brave generation, and a brave man—priceless."*

We all cherish the photo to this day, and I would love to share
it with you here—but cell phone technology and printing aren't
yet compatible. It would reduce to a blur on the page, so you'll have
to picture it in your mind's eye.

I've used this camera a handful of times since then, each time
recording another priceless shot. So you see, I'm not averse to technology—I'm just wary of the misuse of these cell phones. I'm
guessing that for most Road Warriors who travel to Europe, you
manage just fine without your cell phone. Isn't it amazing how
when we leave the country we magically don't have to be on the
phone every waking hour?

Of course, lucky us, the cell phone industry is trying to make the
technology easier and more affordable for those who travel out of
the country. Some cell phones are equipped with the technology to
make those calls from wherever you happen to be; they're called
"world phones," and they're put out by numerous companies.

If you don't own a world phone, you can rent one—but it will
cost you. For instance, Verizon Wireless (800-711-8300) will ship

Verizon customers a phone—but be prepared to pay a per day charge along with an airtime charge. If you frequently travel out of the country, another alternative is buying an international phone. There are companies such as Mobal Rental (www.mobalrental. com), that require no monthly fee or recurring charges and sell phones that work in more than 130 countries. Airtime isn't cheap, so if you plan on making a lot of calls, check out other companies such as Cellular Abroad (www.cellularabroad.com) that charge low home-country rates, plus a weekly or monthly rental fee.

BlackBerry

No doubt you've seen a few of these around. For those who have to be in constant communication, this little device will do just that and then some. If you've ever seen someone intensely staring at their hand, you may very well have seen one. As the folks at Black-Berry themselves say, "It combines award-winning devices, software and services to keep mobile professionals connected to the people, data and resources that drive their day."

Much like a cell phone, a device like this can be badly misused. However, if you promise me you won't bang into me with your suitcase while loading or unloading on the plane, I'll leave you alone while you stare at your hand.

Laptop

Everyone's business is different, and that means the technology carried by each Road Warrior can be different. For me, my laptop computer is the most important device in my bag. I use it for my presentations, and without it, I would not only be out of business, you would not be reading this book. At this point, the pecking order of love for me goes like this: wife, kids, family, friends, pets, laptop. A strange but poignant entry . . .

> **Friday, September 21st–3:30 A.M.**
> I'm not sure at 3:30 A.M. if it's politically correct to call it very late or very early, but here I sit with my friend the laptop in front of me. I've been out all week, traveled to five cities in five days, and logged about 10,000 miles in the air. I'm tired, beat up, and a bit lonely. Most of the time I spend on trips, especially this one, is spent alone. It's kind of weird, but the only constant in my life on the road is this laptop. It works alongside me on my presentations, it helped me write a number of books, it allows me to communicate with my family and clients in the evening, it has allowed me to record through my journals my life on the road, it plays music when I need it, it lets me play when I need to, it shows me pictures of my family when I need them, and has acted as a true companion.

Not everyone can get emotional about a laptop, but most Road Warriors would give up a pinky before giving up their laptop. With that in mind, let's go a bit deeper in the search for the perfect laptop . . . companion.

Size

So, you're looking to add to or upgrade your technology, and you're working on your laptop-shopping list. Be careful; the size of your laptop can become a curse. I learned that the hard way when I became obsessed with the newest, greatest, and of course largest laptop I could find . . .

January 27th—5:30 P.M.

Heading out of the deep freeze of Washington, D.C., which will see a high of 20 degrees, to sunny Phoenix, which is getting up to the mid 80s. I'm actually looking forward to this trip. I'm breaking in my new laptop, a Sony VAIO. It's a bit large, but I like it. I got it to integrate my video with my PowerPoint, and supposedly, this is the best on the market to do just that. What's more, with a whopping 16.1-inch screen, it will be fantastic for watching a movie or two!

Yep, the sweet sounds of blissful ignorance. With that size came two unfortunate side effects. The first was the size itself.

February 25th—9:15 A.M.

I'm on my fifth trip of the year, and the shine has come off the apple, or should I say the laptop. Since 9/11 I have backed myself out of first class and into coach. That's all well and fine if I'm flying United because my miles keep me in the "Premier Zone," but no such luck on some of the other airlines. USAir might be a United "partner" but I'm sure not treated like one. I keep heading south, I keep flying USAir, and they keep putting me 30 rows back. That means no legroom, and no laptop room.

My laptop is so big, I can barely open it when the person in front of me doesn't lean back. If they do lean back, I can't even place it on the folding tray in front of me. Nope, I've spent most of the past month with my massive laptop in my lap. If the tray is out, I don't even have room for a cup of water!

And then there was the weight . . .

April 17th—7:15 A.M.

I'm moving fairly well, but I just can't move around the room like I want to. This morning I woke up with a neck that is still locked up. I'm not in intense pain, I just can't look right without turning my entire body. I have my trusty 16.1-inch screen and laptop to thank. I was getting out of the cab last night, grabbed ahold of my laptop bag, or should I say ball and chain, swung it out, and felt an electric jolt go right up my spine. I'm cursing the day I purchased that laptop. What was I thinking?!

My penance was to lug that laptop around the country for a year. Then I purchased a docking station and gave it to my wife. The next laptop I purchased was, not surprisingly, one of the lightest on the market. As for the screen size, I'm not really sure; I just don't care. I've been on the road for more than twenty-five years and I've yet to watch a movie anyway! When it comes to picking a laptop, cell phone, or any other device, remember one of the oldest Road Warrior sayings, and you'll be just fine.

Travel light—travel bright.

Power

When it comes to laptops, there are two ways to analyze power. The first is the actual speed and capacity of the machine. By the time this book comes out, whatever number I quote you will have doubled. Suffice to say, unless you are running a lot of video, which hogs disk space, the power of the newest and weakest machine should do just fine.

But this is a book dedicated the road, so I want to address the power issue of the actual supply of energy. It sounds like a rather trivial subject, but the fact is, if you don't have the power to run your gear, it's not going to be of much use. In the air the laptop is king—but unfortunately, despite the wild claims made by many of the laptop manufacturers, battery life can be an issue on those longer flights.

November 14–9:15 P.M.

I'm on my way to Las Vegas, and with the limited nonstops from Washington, D.C., I'm connecting through Los Angeles. I charged my laptop battery before the trip, but we were over five hours in the air, and that battery only lasted about three. So, with an hour layover you think I'd have time to put some more juice back into my laptop–but you'd think wrong. It seems that finding an outlet in most airports is like trying to find Waldo. I hovered around the only outlet near my gate, swooped in when one of the two users left, and now have about 20 minutes of battery life left. I'd better type fast!

So if you're looking for an outlet, try my first choice—near the pay phones—but that's iffy at best, and usually scouted out by other Road Warriors. From there, it's anybody's guess. Sometimes I'll find one on a pillar or under a chair against the wall. When I do find one, it's usually one outlet per gate, which can have a couple of hundred people waiting. That means charging up can be a major problem. One thing for sure—it seems that the airlines aren't interested in helping the Road Warriors get powered up for flights.

If it were up to me, I'd simply fix up my airport to keep up with the times. I guess thirty years ago we didn't have any devices but our suitcases to take on board, but that changed a few decades ago. Well, the airports might not be interested in keeping up with our demands, but the aircraft are at least trying with in-seat power.

The industry standard for in-seat power outlets on airplanes is the empower socket, which until recently has been almost exclusively a perk of business and first class. Now this perk is working its way into the coach cabins. Make sure you know how to charge the electronics that help keep you in touch. You'll need to change DC to 120-volt AC via a power inverter such as the iGo Juice (www.igo.com), which plugs into empower sockets, AC outlets, and car lighters and can charge a laptop, PDA, and cell phone simultaneously. Inverters come in various wattage outputs, and most laptops require 70 to 90 watts, so check your computer before buying one. Good information if you are traveling within the country.

February 2nd–6:15 P.M.

Phew, that was a close one! I finished my first day of delivery for Total Gas in London. I was a little nervous about plugging in without a transformer, but my laptop manufacturer and my client both promised me that a simple plug converter would do the trick. When the sparks started flying I reached in and pulled the plug like a lizard snatching a fly. The spokes on my plug were blackened, but no damage was done . . . thank goodness!

Most new laptops and travel-oriented electronics such as digital cameras can run on North American (110–120 volt) or foreign (220–240 volt) standards, eliminating the need for items that convert voltage, but be careful. You never know which of the older devices you might have may still need one. Numerous companies sell adapters that allow you to plug electronics into foreign outlets. These adapters can be purchased individually or in global sets. A foreign surge protector is a good idea for sensitive gear. Some of the more exclusive hotels will even lend transformers and adapters to guests.

Wireless Internet access is spreading quickly, which means business travelers are less likely to have to track down a trendy

Internet cafe. Most major hotel chains offer it—for an additional fee.

Resources

Understanding the various resources available can save you a lot of time and trouble. Even grizzled Road Warriors like me can make mistakes . . .

> ### Monday, October 6th–10:00 A.M.
> It's going to be a long flight to Houston and it's all my fault. Sometimes I can get a little obsessed with trying to get an exit row without carefully studying where that exit row is. I got an exit row on a Boeing 737 on the aisle–what could be better? How about any other seat on the plane!
>
> I am reminded that on a 737 the exit row is the worst row on the plane. Instead of having three seats across, it is the only row that has two seats. That second seat doesn't really show up as a center seat, so it's frequently booked. You are also rewarded with the only seats on the plane that not only don't recline, the armrests are bolted down. Oh, and the legroom is no larger than any other seat on the plane. It seems that all exit rows are not created equal!
>
> The plane is probably one-third open, but there isn't another open aisle seat, and I think I'm the only guy on the plane with a center seat taken. On cue, as I'm writing this, my rather large seatmate just let out a loud snoring snort . . . and a small amount of drool. Not to worry, I'm only trapped in the metal tube for another two hours. Ugh.

Understanding how to use the resources at hand can keep you out of all sorts of trouble, and I've got a few simple Web sites to go to. One of my favorites is www.Airtravel.about.com. At this site you'll not only get a picture of the plane you will be sitting in, and seat maps, you'll get a whole lot more. Airport information, airline phone numbers, airline travel offers, shopping guides, articles, other resources are at your fingertips. The Web site is easy to maneuver around and kept up to date.

Another site I like is www.inc.com/resources/travel. At this site you'll find a travel forum loaded with information from other Road Warriors: opinions on things like best online travel sites, stress-lowering travel tips, security hold-ups, and more. It also has a nice archive of travel articles.

I've got one last site for you, and then I'll move on. At www.airlinequality.com you'll find a slew of unbiased surveys by the passengers themselves. You'll find all kinds of surveys from Best Cabin Staff, Best Airline Alliance, Best Inflight Entertainment, to Best Airline and Best Airport, to mention a few. Frequently they are pulling these numbers from four to five million surveys, so the results appear valid to me.

As I've said throughout, technology can be both a blessing and a curse. Rather than dwell on its misuse, I'd like to leave this chapter on a positive note. Laptops, cell phones, BlackBerrys, and the various resources available on the Web can make the life of the Road Warrior a lot easier, and a lot more productive from a business standpoint. However, more important than that, the technology can go a long way to helping keep Road Warriors and their families in contact with each other and intact. For that reason, and that reason alone, I'll always be a fan of any new technology that might be coming my way.

CHAPTER ELEVEN

9/11

For George

After a decade of journal entries, and countless stories, little did anyone know what was to unfold on September 11th, 2001. It's a story that shocked the world. None of us were spared the pain of the biggest tragedy of the century. Each of us, in our own way, has had to endure the shock, pain, fear, and bewilderment of a moment in history that no one will ever truly be able to comprehend. As for me, the moment began innocently enough . . .

Monday, September 10th–1:35 P.M.

I'm off to pop into Chicago to deliver a presentation for a customer I've done a lot of work for in the past. I'm looking forward to seeing some old friends. Although I may appear to be Mr. Social to those who don't know me, the fact is, I work alone and travel alone, so this is a treat. It's a good life, but occasionally, it can get lonely. The weather just couldn't be more beautiful.

I look back on that entry with a certain sadness. It represents something that all of us had no idea we were about to lose. It represents an end of our innocence.

Tuesday, September 11th–10:30 A.M.

Today, everything changed. How much–I just don't know. Today, terrorists bombed the World Trade Center and the Pentagon.

At 7:15 A.M. I was up, dressed, and in the training room checking on the A.V. equipment. At 7:45 A.M., the news started working its

way through the room. "A plane has hit the World Trade Center!" I
wanted to think it was a tragic accident.

A crowd started forming around the television set in the lobby.
As we watched the flames burning from the first plane, another
plane hit the second building. Now we knew we were under attack.
The crowd started to swell, not believing what we were watching.
At 8:30 A.M., there were now reports of flames in Washington, D.C.
This just couldn't be happening. What's happening to our world?

I then clicked into my own survival mode. I knew my place was
at home with my family. As reports came of all airports being
closed, I began to scramble to try and get a rental car. Fortunately,
one of the participants at the seminar was someone I had worked
with in the past, and one who lived in Richmond, Virginia . . . and
she had a rental car. Now she has a guest. I'm now in my room,
have changed out of my suit, and am preparing for the long drive
home from Chicago.

September 11, 2001, was an unforgettable day for all of us,
including Road Warriors. The stories I later heard were overwhelming. One story of travel truly amazed me. I had delivered
a seminar in San Diego the night before the one in Chicago, and
had met a participant who lived in Raleigh, North Carolina. I
later found out that he too had tried to rent a car and drive
home—from San Diego. That would have been amazing
enough, but within hours on 9/11, all rental cars were booked,
and he was not able to secure one himself. So what did he
do? What only the most dedicated Road Warrior would do to
fight his way home to be with his family. He bought a car and
drove home.

September 11th—3:00 P.M.

We've worked our way through Illinois and Indiana, and are close to Ohio. I have just bid farewell to my driving partner. As strange as this might sound, her husband started driving at 9:00 A.M., and, through the coordination of cell phones, met us along the road. I'm alone now, but stocked up on food and water, and am getting ready to get back on the road.

Everyone reacted differently to the tragedy of that day, and my driving partner's husband was a classic example. Upon hearing the news of the day, he frantically tried to call her. When he could not reach her cell phone he did something out of love that was rather remarkable. He found a babysitter, got in his car in Richmond, Virginia, and set off for Chicago.

When my car mate and her husband finally did hook up by phone, my car mate was furious. "How could he be so stupid?" she bristled. "Why would he do such a thing?" she kept muttering. It took me a while, but I finally got her to understand. This was a man who might not have made the soundest decision of his life, but this was also a man who truly loved his wife.

September 11th—10:30 P.M.

I've come through the tip of West Virginia, crossed into Pennsylvania, back into West Virginia, and finally into Cumberland, Maryland. Riding on fumes, I finally found a gas station to fill up on. Prices are a little high, but nothing like what I saw in Ohio. I saw 50-car lines for $5 gasoline. Here, it's only about 50 cents higher than normal with about ten cars in front of me, but the attendant on the inside told me they are going up a dollar more a gallon at midnight.

Although I was driving in my car and getting nonstop information, I was not in a unique situation. Nonstop information was coming from everywhere, on every radio station, in every town. It just kept coming and coming.

September 11th–11:30 P.M.

Four and a half hours more of information. I'm worn out and worn down. At least, in another couple of hours, I'll be home with my family, but what then? What will I say? I'm not nearly as beat up by the drive as I am by this information. Will the world ever be the same?

The most difficult aspect of this tragedy for many, including me, was the information. It was everywhere at once and it didn't let up. It couldn't let up. The problem was, no one was equipped to cope with it. I for one felt a moral obligation to watch it. This was not a story you could or would want to hide from. Still, the pictures of the planes hitting the towers, the pictures of the towers coming down, and the haunting pictures of the people running, were difficult to hide from.

I have always felt my biggest blessing was to be born with a strong will to make the best of every situation. I literally trained my children to do the same. However, for the first time in my life, I could find absolutely no positive in this situation. As the days wore on, many of us wore down.

Wednesday, September 12th–4:00 P.M.

No destination to speak of, just depression. Most things are closed today, and I'm staying home with the family. On the outside, I'm trying to look calm, but inside, I'm having trouble. I'm just not used

to dealing with this kind of trouble. The airports are still closed.
What will become of my business? What will become of our world?

In addition to the bleak news we were all encountering twenty-four hours a day, most of us were not spared a human connection. Most of us knew someone who knew someone who was directly touched by the tragedy.

Thursday, September 13th–11:30 P.M.
No destination, just more depression. One of the former managers at Xerox I'd worked with on numerous projects was on the Dulles flight that crashed into the Pentagon. He was with his wife heading to Hawaii to disperse the ashes of her father, who'd passed away. I can't get my head to clear and not dwell on what they must have gone through. What were the final moments like for my friend?

My friend's name was George Simmons. I did not know his wife, Diane, well, but I knew George because everyone knew George. He was the most upbeat person I had ever met. In a company like Xerox, which frowned on people who did things differently, George did everything differently. There was never a sterile memo from George, but rather a memo with a smiley face. Every memo I ever received from George had a pasted smiley face stuck on it.

Saturday, September 15th–6:00 P.M.
I attended a service for my friend George, and have not responded well. I've just never experienced a depression like this in my life.

It's like a wave is building, larger and larger, and I'm inside this wave. It has become more and more difficult.

There is no getting away from the news and the pain. I have always been a person whose greatest strength was his ability to block pain. I just can't block this. I have been withdrawn, and somewhat mean to the children in particular.

I owe a lot to my friend George. He was kind to me when he was alive, but may have given me the greatest gift of all when he was gone. He reminded me to live again. With that said, I have written these three goals and put them in a place in my office that only I can see. They read:

- *I'm going to lead again.*
- *I'm going to instill calm in my family.*
- *I'm going to take care of my family professionally.*

In short, I'm going to stop feeling sorry and start living again. Life can be good again.

Even after George left this earth, he gave me one final gift. He left me with his motto, which I once found somewhat corny. "Life is good." When I pulled up to his house, where the service was being held, I joined more than three hundred other people who were paying their respects. His children helped us all with a sign they had placed on the roof of the house. This sign covered the entire roof of a very large house, and had to be at least a hundred feet long and fifty feet wide. It had a giant yellow smiley face with the words "Life is good" stretching the length of the sign. Most people showed up in Hawaiian shirts, another reflection of who this man was.

From that day on, things were much better at home. Every business was affected in its own way, and mine was no exception. I had $75,000 worth of seminars canceled, but as painful as that was, part of me was glad I wasn't traveling. Eventually, like everyone else, I had to go back up in the air.

Tuesday, September 18th—9:00 A.M.

This is so much harder than I expected. I've been true to my word and have stopped moping in front of the family, but I'm not OK yet. I'm trying to limit my television watching of the crisis, although each time I check in, it's just horrible.

I have a trip to Vancouver coming up in two days and I'm spooked. I've got to get stronger and I've got to get back up on the horse again and fly. It's a nightmare that no one can wake up from. I can't sleep and my mood has gone from spooked to scared.

Thursday, September 20th—7:30 A.M.

I'm in the air. It's very strange. I woke up a couple of times last night, but got some sleep. So much has changed. I had lunch with my parents yesterday thinking it could be the last time I saw them. Most of me knows that there is little chance of me being in the next plane that has a problem, but most of us believe there will be another plane, and there will be more casualties.

I've done my best to be positive in front of the kids, but this only deepens my fear when I am alone. Amazingly, like having a sixth sense and being connected to me, it is only Danny, my son, who has picked up on it. He was following me around last night much like Maggie or Jake (my dogs)—not saying much, just following. He seemed to want to take as many looks at me as possible, and when he wasn't looking at me, I was doing the same thing and staring at him.

I grappled with leaving a note just in case the unspeakable occurs. In an eerie moment in time, I took my Ironman medal off, placed it in an envelope with the note, and left it with my things in my closet. If something were to happen to me, I would want Danny to have it.

I teach people every day that the biggest fear most everyone has is fear of the unknown. The difficulty that the airlines were facing in those first couple of weeks back in operation was just that. The world had changed, and it was our turn, the army of Road Warriors, to change with it.

Friday, September 21st—2:45 P.M.

I'm on board and heading home from Vancouver, and it wasn't easy. One way of observing my condition is to look at my neck. I'm in quite a bit of pain, obviously from stress, but damn it, I did my job, and I'm on board flying home.

I'm having a martini, which is like chugging straight vodka, and I have another on the way. I'm figuring I might be able to loosen up my neck, but I think I just want to be drunk right now. I'm not sure I've ever been drunk on a plane so today might be my first time.

In the morning, as the meeting kicked off, they went around the room and talked about the tragedy that had occurred. Some people cried and it was very moving. I chose not to speak at that time.

When I started my seminar I mentioned that I had a friend who had been on the Dulles flight—my friend George Simmons and his wife—and I said that I had not done a seminar since the tragedy. Then, and I had no idea I would say this, I blurted out I was dedicating the talk to George. It got quiet, I got choked up, but proceeded on.

I thought about George a lot during the talk. When it was over, I thanked them and then tried to get out the words, "I hope you enjoyed it, George." I didn't do a very good job because I was immediately choked up again. Still, I got it said and am thrilled I was able to offer this to my fallen friend. I hope you enjoyed it, George. Rest in peace.

In my twenty-two years of professional speaking, that may very well have been one of my best. I had George with me and that made things a whole lot easier. Once the dust settled, and more Road Warriors and travelers took to the air, the changes that were made out of necessity began to present themselves. Early on, it was difficult for everyone. Arriving two hours before a flight was cutting it close. Curbside baggage check-in was canceled for a while. This didn't bother your local Road Warriors because we don't check our luggage, but your average traveling family sure didn't like it much. Security lines are like a slot machine. You just never know. Sometimes they look like a line at Disney with switchbacks and long waits. These can still be found in many airports early in the morning. The soldiers with rifles and bomb-sniffing dogs are gone . . . at least from our eyesight. I could go on, but suffice to say, changes will continue to evolve, and no matter what travel disruptions they may create, they are being created to help ensure our safety, and that works for me. As we settle into our new, post–9/11 era, the process begins to define itself . . .

Tuesday, June 4, 2002–2:00 P.M.
I've run about a mile with my bags, I'm sweating, I'm out of breath, and I hate to say this, but it feels wonderful. It turns out that 9/11 taught us a lot, including appreciating some of the things we were

too spoiled to be grateful for. For me, I now remember fondly the thrill of running through airports, and catching flights by the skin of my teeth. Ah, the good old days!

My flight was scheduled for 12:15 P.M., in the middle of the day, when most security lines are at their shortest. I was right, and they were. Five minutes later I was on the run to my gate. Five minutes after that I was at my gate. Leaving Oakbrook one hour before my flight was to take off, I made it to the gate with 33 minutes to spare. I even had enough time to slip in line, load with the pre-ferred flyers, and make sure my bags got on. What a performance! Five minutes later, I found out I had more Road Warrior perform-ance to go.

I was thrilled to see my flight was one of the few that was run-ning on time despite heavy rain and thunder at O'Hare. What I didn't expect was for United to give my plane away. The weather was so bad, the 9:15 A.M., 10:15 A.M., and 11:15 A.M. flights had yet to depart. Although the airline had my 12:15 P.M. on time, and the oth-ers showing two-hour delays, that was just an airline gimmick. My flight was never going to be on time. Our plane was now two more flights away, all the other Washington National and Washington Dulles flights were sold out, and with severe weather on the way, United was now telling us to probably look for a hotel. This was at 11:45 A.M.!

I studied the board and noticed a three-hour-delayed Balti-more-Washington International flight loading and planning for a 12:00 P.M. departure. I got the sweat glands moving and made a run for it. As I ran down the C terminal at O'Hare, I heard the last call announcement. I got there just in time, and with the big airports' planes hopelessly sold out, I got a row to myself. In I slid, on I went, and off we flew.

*After I landed at BWI, I checked the O'Hare flights. The severe
weather did move in, forcing five- and six-hour delays. My original
flight was not as fortunate, and was canceled, making my little
maneuverings all the sweeter! There's nothing like watching a
good plan come together just right.*

So, what did we learn with this little story? Plenty. Here's a
recap:

1. It's basic, but needs to be said over and over again. Pack
   light, and get your belongings into two bags. One a carry-
   on that fits the airline requirements, and the other a suitcase
   that does the same. If you pack intelligently, you can still
   take five days' worth of clothes in that suitcase, and that
   includes suits.

2. Avoid the check-in lines; use the kiosk machines instead.
   Most of the major airports where the worst lines are have
   them.

3. If possible, plan your trips around midday. With fewer
   flights and plenty of airplanes, even if your plane has a
   mechanical problem, most airports can find another that
   can fill in and take you where you need to go. Security lines
   are almost nonexistent at these times.

4. Stop taking your car to the airport, and use a taxi. If you are
   in Washington, D.C., you can use Sam, my driver. He'd love
   your business. If not, find a Sam in your city. This will allow
   you the flexibility to make the changes necessary to get
   home, and that often means switching arrival airports.

5. Speaking of arrival airports, don't forget the less-traveled
   airports that are less traveled because they usually aren't as
   convenient. For me, BWI is thirty minutes farther away than

National and Dulles. However, when every other flight is canceling back to your home, leaving the remaining flights way oversold, it's nice to have a BWI in your hip pocket, and BWI is not the only airport that bails Road Warriors like me out. In Houston, there's Hobby, in Chicago, there's Midway, and the list goes on and on.

Security will continue to tighten, and passengers will continue to comply. No one believes that the war against terrorism will ever really end. Yet we as a society push on. And Road Warriors—we continue to adapt to the changes within our industry. We embrace these changes, for without them, we can no longer exist as professionals.

So, to those who wish to harm innocent people in the name of a God who surely agonizes over your misinterpretations, I pity your souls. God bless America.

CHAPTER TWELVE

Overcoming the Addiction

So there you are. You've read the stories, and with a little luck, you've learned something from the lessons. However, there is one more lesson to go. It is a lesson in the ultimate survival of the Road Warrior. Significant dangers apply to anyone who, on a consistent basis, sacrifices family for work. This type of Road Warrior is really nothing more than a workaholic who conducts work away from home.

I recognize the fact that we all encounter times when we must do things we don't want to do. What's more, I think this is a phase that most who work and travel must go through. I refer to it as "cracking rocks." Like a convict from a century ago, sometimes you must do things that are meaningless and painful. It's almost like a rite of passage, and when it comes to professional travel, some jobs require a period of time where you just have to go out and crack some rocks. Sorry to sound like your dad, but in a sense, it's good for you.

No, I'm not talking about that kind of Road Warrior travel, now. I'm talking about years later, when that same Road Warrior is *still* cracking those rocks. It's a dirty job cracking rocks, but it's often necessary—and many a company that finds people who crack rocks well and don't complain about it will eagerly allow them the privilege of doing it until they die.

These are the stories of the pain, destruction, and addiction that permeate the lives of so many Road Warriors. These are the confessions of one Road Warrior who knows the downfall of too much travel, the destruction it can create, and, thank God, the road to recovery.

Let's start with an entry that isn't mine, but a fellow Road Warrior I met once who told me his story . . .

A Wakeup Call

It was my 27th wedding anniversary; and, as usual, I was traveling. I was able to get an earlier flight from Nashville to surprise my wife and celebrate. I had bought a gold bracelet, a dozen roses, and a card and arrived home around 6:30 P.M. to find no one there.

I thought to myself "I should have called" but figured she would be home shortly. Wrong! She finally got home around 10:15 P.M. I gave her the gifts and said "Happy Anniversary," to which she replied, "I am not going to acknowledge this one. I want a separation. You have been consumed by your work and there is and has been no place for the girls and me in your life." You could have shot me with a submachine gun and I would not have been more shocked! What a wake-up call!

Living alone over the next three and a half years and with the help of my rector, a psychologist, a psychiatrist, and a marriage counselor, I was able get my priorities back in order as to the important, meaningful, and real things in life. A career in commercial banking, investment banking, and working for a Fortune 500 corporation had muddled my mind into believing that the real values in life were how much money you made, the physical structure of your home, the cars you drove, the clothes you wore, being seen at the country club, acquiring the play toys associated with success and wealth, and, by all means, Achieving Million Mile Status! What bunk!

My workaholism almost cost me my family, but I have, and continue to, put things back in perspective: God first; Family second; My Fellow Man third; Job fourth, and Me last. And I am happy to say I have my wife and family back! Things are certainly not perfect, but we are working on them.

—Name Withheld

The Road Warrior Addiction

Now that I have given away the secrets on how to win on the road, I have a confession to make: I am now a recovering Road Warrior. I have an addiction that is very complicated. It involves money, freedom, and personal success. I believe it is my moral obligation to expose the realities of this problem that now plagues our society. Let me start by telling you how this addiction occurred.

When I left Xerox, I left for a couple of reasons. One of the most significant reasons was the enormous travel I was being asked to endure. At the risk of sounding ignorant, I was good at what I did, and the corporation knew it. The corporation also knew that it had every legal right to exploit my talents, and it did.

I spent years on the road, traveling and being a good corporate soldier. When asked about my tremendous travel schedule, I responded the way a corporate soldier is supposed to respond, "There's nothing I can do about it, honey, I have to do what Xerox tells me to do."

Finally, I decided that I did not have to do what Xerox told me to do, and I left. It's important to note that the single biggest reason why I left was because I was asked to be away from my family too much.

I had decided there was something I could do about all of my travel, and I did it. One day, I shocked the corporation and walked away from it all. I hung a shingle in front of my new office and pursued the great American dream. I went into business for myself.

Of course, every business has a start-up period, so the first year I was given carte blanche to travel as I pleased. I believe the real addiction started there. Then something even worse happened. I became successful.

It isn't rare at all for Road Warriors to be paid well for their travels. It's really quite a deal when you think about it. Sacrifice your family, and you make a lot of money. When I look back at my decision to leave Xerox, I don't think it was all that brave. The money really wasn't that good, and neither were the work conditions.

When I opened up my own consulting business, I began to make an obscene amount of money, and the addiction grew stronger.

Friday, September 19th—5:25 A.M.

The week is finally over. Washington, D.C., to San Francisco. San Francisco to Houston. Houston to Denver. Up to Key Stone. Back to Denver. Over to Aspen. Back to Denver. Now, mercifully, Denver to home. It's a crude measurement, but I made in this one week what it would have taken me almost four months to make at Xerox. I would have loved to have seen any trainer from Covey to Hopkins, Zigler to Tracy, try and match my performance level. I love this business!

There's no doubt about it, the money can be intoxicating. I suppose most addictions do control their victims with these types of illusions. I not only liked the money I was making, I loved the power that went with it. It gave me a buzz like alcohol, and I liked the way my travel drug made me feel.

Monday, June 22nd–1:30 A.M.

I love New York. As par for the course, when I landed, there was the Jolles sign held by a limo driver. I got into my stretch and headed into Manhattan. Once in the city, I met up with one of my clients, went to Morton's for a wonderful steak, and then smoked a Cuban cigar for dessert. This is as good as it gets.

Quite quickly, my business began to grow. Now I loved the power, the money, and the limos. I couldn't imagine being happier in my work. Everything was working perfectly—except for one thing—my family was suffering.

Friday, February 14th–1:30 P.M.

I was treated as an invited guest of NASA and saw the launch of Discovery, the space shuttle. What a thrill that was. I hung out with the engineers and inside people, sat in the VIP section, and watched night become day at 3:50 A.M. It was bright, loud, and fast. I feel fortunate to have been there.

What a week. It seems incomprehensible to me that within the past two weeks I have gone from watching a 3:40 A.M. Discovery space rocket liftoff at Cape Canaveral to lunching on a ship floating down the Nile in Cairo, Egypt. The only problem is, I couldn't share this with my family.

My business was getting bigger, my bookings were off the chart, the money was tremendous, and the accolades were piling up. Never in my wildest dreams did I think my ability to speak would take me to the heights they were taking me.

Sunday, September 9th–10:30 P.M.

I've got something to tell the kids on this one. Seems the keynote was previously booked for another speaker–some guy named Bill Clinton. Our ex-president was booked and ready to go until the meeting planners announced the great news to their constituency. Then all hell broke loose.

I was told of the 300 letters that were sent out, 275 were greeted with cheers or apathy. It's the other 25 they had problems with. Those 25 raised such a stink with letters, threats, and complaints they were forced to cancel him . . . and his $110,000 speaking fee. That's where I came in.

In a sense, I got the ex-president's leftovers. I didn't exactly get his speaking fee, but I'm going to be paid extremely well for this one! What a neat opportunity to keynote a meeting like this and have the distinction of taking over for my man Bill. Who would ever have thought that the little left-handed kid from Silver Spring, Maryland, would someday fill in for the former president of the United States?!

I have never had a problem with alcohol, but I have studied what's known as "the twelve steps" that are suggested for personal recovery. A number of the steps have religious references, which I will not mention. But many of the other steps apply well to an addiction to work on the road that plagues so many in this country.

For instance, the first of the twelve steps is to admit how unmanageable the power of the addiction has become. I knew something wasn't right, but I was unwilling to admit that I had no control over what I was doing. I would preach to anyone who would listen, "I plan on slowing it down, soon."

As addictions claim the souls of their victims, they become carriers of neglect and denial. I refused to believe I was harming my family. After all, in my mind, I was providing for them in an extraordinary fashion. They got everything they wanted—clothes, gifts, trips—you name it. They got everything but *me*.

In a sense, I became a prisoner of my own success. It's funny. Every male child gets a lot of lessons that have to do with success. They all teach the same thing. "Keep reaching, keep striving, and never give up. Be the best that you can be." It's a seductive message, and one we would like to believe. The problem is, it's not true.

There is no course that teaches us how high is high enough. I always assumed that if a rung of a ladder presented itself, you just grabbed it and climbed. I was wrong. I went into a heavy denial stage.

Saturday, 19th—10:00 P.M.

I'm heading back from Dallas, and boy, did I clean up on that seminar. I had a customer approach me to do a Saturday seminar, and I'm quite proud to report, I turned them down. The problem was, they didn't know how to take "no" for an answer.

They asked me for my speaking fee, and when I told them I'm out most of the week and don't like to conduct a Saturday seminar, they offered me a thousand dollars more. When I told them that it would mean I would have to miss my daughter's soccer game, they offered me two thousand more. Three thousand more

*on top of my regular speaking fee for an hour seminar! I grabbed
it. Jessie was upset, but we'll be able to buy a lot of soccer balls
with this little bonus. I'll make it up to her.*

I'm ashamed of that entry, but it needs to be seen. I sold out
that day—and on too many others. I put a dollar figure on my
child's happiness. This addiction runs deep, and the denial runs
deeper. To give you a better sense of how twisted the logic can
become to placate the denial, I present you with this bit of Road
Warrior logic.

Friday, March 22nd—9:00 P.M.
*I've been out a lot this month, but you know what? I think I'm a
better father because of it. When I'm away, it's a little rough, but
that all changes when I get home. Because of my time away, I'm
so happy to see my kids, I'm a tremendous father. I can't wait to
play with them.*

In my years as a Road Warrior, I have seen the ravages that the
road can bring. I have seen the infidelity and the alcoholism. Alcohol rots the liver. Excessive travel rots the family. I have seen what
Thoreau has written about. I have seen the Road Warriors who live
their lives of "quiet desperation."

This quiet desperation can be deadly. It isolates its victims due
to the sheer number of days and nights the Road Warrior must be
away. It can make good people behave very badly.

Tuesday, July 15th—4:45 P.M.
*I met a man today who turned my stomach. We started talking
about all the travel, and the hotels, and he started to smile. He*

*reached for his bag, and proudly pulled out two items. With a grin
and a wink, this married man told me it was his "Hotel Survival Kit."
Inside were two items—a stethoscope and hospital scrubs. He
smugly told me this was how he dressed for the bars at night.*

I truly felt pity for this man, but even more so for his family.
What a sad situation. Despite his smile, I could only imagine the
sorrow and the shame he should have felt, and if somewhere down
deep inside he didn't feel ashamed, he would someday. With that
said, I would feel even worse for the family he deceived.

The affliction takes its toll not only on the Road Warrior but
on the family as well. In addition, it's not just the children or the
wife who are affected by this isolation. It's the friends, and for that
matter, anyone who tries to get close to the Road Warrior. After a
while, the act of denial can no longer sustain the Road Warrior.
Eventually, doubt creeps in.

Thursday, May 29th—2:45 P.M.

*I'm struggling with my emotions this week, and it's difficult for me
to admit it. I'm probably in the worst traveling run of the year, and
it's taking its toll. My energy is a little low, and in my own pathetic
way, I'm kind of homesick. I miss Ronni, I miss the kids, I miss the
dogs, I miss my bed.*

*The tough part may be yet to come. I'm really not feeling that
well, and when I walk in that door at home, I'm going to have to
ignore any pain I feel and tend to Ronni's pain. I don't know what
that is, yet, but I've come to accept a kind of rule of thumb. "The
harder my week and the more pain it created in me, the more I
must give to Ronni." I've stopped whining about it and have
accepted it as a given.*

It is almost impossible for the Road Warrior to understand that the week at home endured by the family could possibly be more difficult than the week on the road. The delays, the cancellations, the ups and the downs of life on the road fuel a selfish assumption that no one's life could be more difficult.

What we don't understand is that the void created by our absence forces families to function as single-spouse entities. The driving to soccer practice, after-school events, and birthday parties are only some of the chores that the spouse left behind must perform alone. The homework, the trips to the bus stop, and even dinner become tedious chores. The family unit is dysfunctional.

The struggle is overwhelming. There is a strange vulnerability to being a Road Warrior. This vulnerability does not lie in what many would think would be the obvious area of travel. That may be demanding, but in a way, it's predictable.

No, the real struggle lies within. With travel comes success. Often, the greater the travel, the greater the success. However, the greater the success, the greater the damage suffered by the family left behind. This is the same family the Road Warrior is working so hard to support. It's a troubling quirk of fate.

Friday, July 5th—10:30 P.M.

When the work is through, I take a 7:30 P.M. flight to Los Angeles so I can wait for the 10:00 P.M. flight (really 1:00 A.M. East Coast time) to fly all night and land at home at 5:35 A.M. Oh boy. Some weekend. Sadly, Ronni seems to think this is appealing to me, and that I enjoy this. This is how I make my living. If I give in to the depression, I fail. There is no one there to catch me, I simply become another casualty of the road. Sometimes, I think if I let it get me down more and show it, Ronni will be happier. I can't turn it on and then off again. If I do, I may not be able to turn it off. As a professional speaker, that would be the end.

It's a terrible addiction. At least with alcohol, you are either drinking or you are not drinking. With a travel addiction, no matter how many customers you say "no" to, there will always be some travel. Imagine trying to stop drinking with the understanding that there is always going to be a little drinking. What makes the situation even more difficult is the fact that being home doesn't necessarily make everything right. After a long, tedious trip, it's difficult to walk through the door, switch hats, and be ready to manage the home.

Thursday, October 24th—9:50 A.M.

What a difference 12 hours makes! I had no idea how tired I was until I got home. I walked through the door and was assaulted by Danny and Jessie. Daisy (the dog) soon followed, and Ronni was right behind. I went in to say good night to Sandy and then began to unpack. As I was unpacking, Ronni began to go over a written list of issues that had come up since I had left. There were seven. I overdosed at five. After being buried by the list, I had to jump in the car and go back to the office. I picked up the necessary items for this trip and went home again. Then I packed my bag for today's trip.

The emotional pain brought on by a life on the road is plain to see. But that's not the only damage it can do. There is physical pain to contend with, also. You've heard me complain about my neck. The years on the road did nothing to improve my condition. It wasn't unusual for me to come home unable to look to my left, dehydrated, and with slight muscle twitches under my right eye.

For me, I sensed it was coming to an end a couple of years ago. Although I maintained my disciplined approach of not letting doubt creep into my mind, it didn't stop me from seeing the pain on the faces of my Road Warrior friends.

Thursday, April 10th–7:45 A.M.

I spoke after lunch today in beautiful Palm Springs. The funny thing is, today it didn't look so beautiful. My contact person has become a friend of mine. I have known him through the years, and we have swapped travel stories. He travels more than I do. What a stud. Today, however, he was so stressed, he became ill. Noticeably and seriously ill. He was led away to bed five minutes before I was to speak. It shook me up, and I had trouble getting it out of my head. His pale, fragile look reminded me of the looks I saw at Xerox. The looks of people being pushed too hard. The look of someone who had lost perspective. Perhaps what really scared me was that occasionally, when I was at Xerox, that look stared back at me in the mirror.

I did my best, but I worked this room looking like an injured animal. I even finished my three hours with a talk about working a presentation as hard as you could, even when you are having problems and are not at your best. I was talking about me.

The physical pain, the emotional pain, the pain my children were experiencing with a part-time dad, and the pain I was creating in my marriage finally caught up with me. I was racked with guilt, but I blocked the pain so I could function as a Road Warrior and do my job like a good soldier. For me, it all came crashing down one night in July. I had come off the road from a vicious trip, but also from a vicious couple of months. When I came home, my wife sat me down.

Friday, July 25, 1997–11:45 P.M.

Tonight marks the most significant entry I have ever made in the seven years I have kept this journal. After a brutal conversation with Ronni, a change in business is in order. As the ultimate optimist, I can no longer ignore reality. My marriage is not working. My children are growing up without me. I can no longer wait until next month. It is time to make a few changes.

When I left Xerox, I left because I was not spending enough time with my family. I claimed it was a family decision, and in a way, it was. I was also frustrated professionally.

I am traveling more than when I was with Xerox. I have been blinded, however, by the financial success of my business. The money has been there, and I have been taking it. Well, maybe I have taken a little too much. A lot of what I take is not critical for us to live on—it's just there for the taking. So, here's the new plan:

- *I will conduct no more than four, one-day-or-less seminars a month!*
- *I will commit myself to find trainers to work for me and conduct seminars for me.*
- *I will work harder at generating local business.*
- *I will find other ways to generate money.*
- *I will be a better husband.*
- *I will be a better father.*
- *I will be a better friend.*

That's the plan. I will put all of my heart into this plan. Part of me is happy, because I know those around me will benefit. Part of me is sad, because I am basically ending my opportunity to be the best at what I do. With the new formula, that will be impossible. That's a fact, and I have to live with it. It is a little foreign for me not to try my hardest at something, but in a sense, that's what I will be doing.

I will have the memory, however, of being one of the best damn trainers in the country. That will have to be enough. Now I'm going to be one of the best damn human beings in the country.

This is the end of an era—my era. I know that I will never be able to be the best at what I do, because of the sacrifice I will be making. You can't succeed on a part-time basis. I am battling my instinct to compete and be the best. I am prepared to give this up, now. The strangest thing is, the moment I realized what my decision had to be, I felt a tremendous release of tension. Then I did something that completely caught me by surprise. I left the room and went downstairs, because I didn't want my wife to see me crying.

That was the night I came to grips with my life as a Road Warrior and the addiction that gripped my life. Again, I refer to this as an addiction, because I know that no matter what plan I lay out, and how careful I am, controlling my desire for success is always essential. Many books are written about achieving success, but very little is written about how to cope with it and who potentially suffers from it. We all know that you must sacrifice to be successful, but how much sacrifice is enough, and how successful is "successful enough"?

I did not write a book for the Road Warrior as a way to criticize the Road Warrior. It is a fraternity of which I am, and always will be, a member. I want to discuss the survival, however, of human beings in precarious positions. I know for many who are reading this, it seems there is little that can be done. Perhaps a manager or corporation is controlling your time. I have certainly been there. It would be hypocritical of me to tell you not to listen. I did, but I paid for it. I'm not telling you to go in and shout, "I'm mad as hell, and I'm not going to take it anymore." I'm telling you that if you want to beat this addiction, or want to help someone beat this addiction, I believe I can help. There is hope, and there are ways to survive.

The Solution

If your travel is seemingly out of your hands, I'm here to tell you that, in fact, it is very much within your control. One of the twelve steps in AA says to make "a searching and fearless moral inventory" of ourselves. Well, I believe a corresponding step is to take your search to the mirror, and ask yourself these questions.

Are you being controlled by your job? It's not an easy question, and the honest answer takes courage. No one wants to admit to not being in control of life.

As I mentioned earlier in this chapter, it is natural for a period of time to give your all to a particular job. The employment interview process would be fairly quick if the answer to the question about giving it all to your job was answered with anything but a resounding "Yes!"

However, there needs to be a beginning, middle, and an end to letting your job control your life. This doesn't happen by chance.

You won't find this path written out in the Welcome to the Corporation manual given to you by Personnel.

Wednesday, July 12th–7:30 P.M.

What a sad conversation. I just got off a flight here to Atlanta and got into a conversation with a fellow Road Warrior. I've always felt that my two million miles in the air are fairly impressive. This guy flies close to a million miles a year! His commute is from London to California, and he has been doing this for five years.

I then had to ask him how his family felt about it, and his answer was fairly predictable. He told me he's almost always home on the weekends, so he doesn't miss his visitations.

No job is worth that kind of loss. Admitting to the problem is half the battle. The other half of the battle is committing to do something about it. When you consider what's often at stake, making this change shouldn't be as difficult as it might sound.

Is the travel really out of your control? This was something I preached for years and years while working for Computer Sciences Corporation and Xerox. "There's nothing I can do about this travel! It's out of my control!" In retrospect, that wasn't quite true. These companies liked what I did on the road, but so did I. If I had ever approached them and told them how damaging the long-term travel was, I believe we could have negotiated a solution.

It was more convenient to hit the road and blame the company. This became a little more obvious to me when I went into business for myself. The company was me, and the boss was me. I did not like leaving my family, but then again, I did not mind the time alone, the accolades, and the money. No, in retrospect, I was—and always have been—in more control than I thought.

Are there creative alternatives for managing your travel? When you first analyze this situation, it appears to be such a black-and-white issue. Either you travel and abandon your family, or you don't. But you do have other alternatives. For instance, if you are a Road Warrior who regularly leaves your family or friends, why can't you take them with you from time to time?

> **Friday, August 22nd—9:55 A.M.**
> I'm on my way to West Palm Beach, Florida, and I have a little guest. Danny (my son), is by my side for this trip. I will be speaking to NationsBank this afternoon, and then it's playtime until we leave in the morning. Now, a word from Danny:
> "Well this will be good. After he is done, well let's say, we'll be making some trips. The toy store would be nice. Mini golfing, maybe. Right now, I'm a bit frightened. If I do die, I'll die with my dad. Daddy, you can take over."
> Nice, comforting words from Danny! Anyway, I'll be a lot more relaxed once the seminar is over. It sure is nice to have a friend with me, though.

Once a year, I take each one of my children with me on a trip. Doing this helps out the travel problem in a couple of ways. First, it allows for some good, strong bonding time. When you take one of your children on a trip for a few days, you can get to a level of intimacy and understanding that I'm really not sure you could ever achieve on a daily basis at home. There's no Nintendo, or television, or the other distracting routines found at home. It's just you and them.

There is one other advantage. I believe my children benefited from traveling with their Road Warrior father. They gain a true understanding of what their father actually does. I know when I grew up, I truly didn't know what my father did until I was about fifteen years old. I didn't understand how he did what he did until I was about twenty-five years old.

I recognize that not every Road Warrior can take children to critical meetings and other events. However, in a year of travel, I can't believe for a minute that you don't have at least a trip or two where you really could take them with you.

The costs associated with implementing this idea are negligible when you think about the airline miles you've accumulated that can be redeemed for free travel. Most of the travel expenses are already paid for. Speaking from firsthand knowledge, it is amazing how much my children look forward to these trips, and how much more understanding they are when their dad is on the road.

How are you defining success? I believe that to fight this addiction, you must gain a better understanding of true success. For me and many other Road Warriors, success meant making as much money as possible. The dictionary even defines success as "the attainment of wealth, favor, or eminence." With all due respect to Mr. Webster, I'm not so sure I agree with that definition. My definition of success no longer contains the emphasis it previously had on *wealth*. My definition of success is now "the harmonious balancing of job, family, friends, and health."

I've heard it said by a few people in my life that monetary achievements just aren't as important as we are led to believe. Has anyone ever been quoted on their death bed as saying, "If only I could have made some more money and spent more time away from the family, I would have been so much happier!" The reality is quite the opposite.

Soon after my change in travel schedule, I met another man in a small town in Michigan who provided me with a quote that I keep up in my office to this day.

Thursday, September 13th–4:00 P.M.

I met a fascinating individual named Jerry Harte who spoke after me. He is a training consultant who conducts motivational seminars on positive thinking. He gave me his book, and in a brief conversation, I took an immediate liking to him. He seemed at peace with himself. I thumbed through his book. It is short and to the point. It also has some motivational gems. This one has stuck with me. I think I'm going to enlarge this phrase and put it in my office:

> We were not put on this earth to make a living.
> We were put on this earth to make a difference.

What measurable goals have you established? A critical change I would recommend for Road Warriors is to set a goal for controlling the travel addiction. Now, when I talk about a goal, I don't mean the types of goals I set for fifteen years. Believe it or not, I used to write out my goals and keep them with me. The problem was, my goals were not measurable. While I was in my denial stages of work addiction, one of the goals I kept for a number of years actually said, "Gain control over my travel." Great goal. The only problem was, I never did anything about it.

Make your goal a measurable one. Ask yourself, and your family if you have one, "How many nights out a month would be tolerable?" For me, the number was four. I have some months where

I am above that number and some months where I am below that number, but the number four rules my calendar.

I can't stress enough how important a measurable goal is. If you have had a good month while achieving your travel goal, terrific. If you have had a bad month and exceeded your travel goal, what are you going to do about it? The key is, when someone asks you how you are managing your travel, you can answer them with a measurement.

Sometimes I take my medicine all in one dose and travel the whole week. My family knows, however, that I will not be traveling for the rest of the month. Although they miss me, it is not nearly as hard on them. Just remember this. Without a measurement, you have no real control over your goals. When you can measure it, you can fix it.

Are you maximizing your time at home? A Road Warrior fights the planes, the trains, the hotels, and the cabs, all to make a living and do a job. Back at home, the real work begins.

Frequently, when I walk through the door, the last thing I want to do is play soccer. Too bad, because if you and your family are going to survive the life of the Road Warrior, you'd better stretch out before you open that door. Symbolically, what that means is that doing the job at home and on the road isn't easy, but it's worth it.

Putting in that little extra time pays huge dividends to your loved ones. It also pays dividends to you. Another of the twelve steps suggests you should make a list of all persons you have harmed and become willing to make amends to them. You will most likely not have to look further than those who are waiting up for you when you get home.

Sunday, February 1st–7:15 P.M.

Sam picked me up from the Pan Am Shopping Center before I headed off to New York this evening. He picked me up from the Discovery Zone, where we celebrated my little Sandy's fifth birthday. It was a sweet little party. It is giving me a warm feeling thinking about it. I had to give up the cushy nonstop I had booked, leave late, and get into Dallas late tonight. It was an easy decision, because I'm not missing another birthday ever again. Travel can be rough, but leaving from an event like that makes it a whole lot better.

Every minute is precious to the Road Warrior. Making it home before bedtime, making it to the bus stop before flying out, or simply being there for a Valentine's Day goes a long way toward surviving life on the road.

When you think about it, the changes that need to be made by Road Warriors aren't that horrible. I know that I had many fears. What I failed to realize was that—in addition to my wife, children, and friends—someone else would benefit from my decision to slow it all down. That someone was me.

Thursday, August 13th–1:00 P.M.

I'm off to one of my favorite spots in the world, today. I'm off to Aspen, Colorado. One thing nice about not traveling as much is that I don't have the guilt I had last year. That transfers into an occasional quality trip like the one I'm taking today. I don't speak until tomorrow—and are you ready for this? I'm actually spending the night tomorrow and leaving early Friday morning.

When you remove the guilt from business travel, it becomes enjoyable again. My health has been better, and my attitude has been better. My kids even say it's kind of nice having me on the road a couple of nights a month. As my son said the other day, when we spoke of my travel, "I don't have to tie my shoes or clean my room a couple of days a month!"

Are you prepared to fail? When you set a goal to reduce the contact time you are accustomed to spending on the road with your customers, you must be prepared to fail. I did not make the changes I did because I believed I would be more successful. As a matter of fact, I fully expected to work much harder and be rewarded by failing more frequently. I haven't been disappointed. As for my customers, some have accepted it . . .

Wednesday, February 25th—7:30 P.M.

You know, I'm getting more and more comfortable with the changes I have made in my business. It's amazing what you can accomplish if you just ask. I'm on my way to New York this morning to conduct a one-hour seminar. It had originally been scheduled for 9:00 A.M. to 10:00 A.M. That would have required me to fly in the night before. When the meeting planner asked if that was OK, I hesitantly told her, "No." I told her that if I could speak right before lunch, I would be able to coach a soccer practice for my daughter the night before.

She not only rescheduled my speaking slot for 11:00 A.M., she told me she had kids and thought it was wonderful where I had placed my priorities. She would make sure that whenever I was scheduled as a speaker, she would be sensitive to my speaking time. What's even more amazing, this is the second time this week I have been complimented for wanting to change my speaking slot. There's a lesson here.

And some have not accepted it . . .

Friday, December 4th–5:20 P.M.

This year is closing with a bang. It looks like my role with a big client is going to grow larger next year. However, my role with one of my other large customers appears to be shrinking. The latter is a disturbing development that I just can't seem to alter. There is a lot of infighting going on within the company, and each day appears to be moving me closer to being a casualty.

I believe a lot of what appears to be moving us apart is caused by a lack of commitment by me from my reduced travel schedule. I'm hearing, on the sly, that this policy is making the company uncomfortable. Most likely, it's making those uncomfortable whose families were broken apart because they did not see the warning signs. If they can't accept the fact that my family is more important, it's just as well we part as friends.

As I bare my soul here, I must tell you that giving up the fortune and fame that was at my fingertips has not always been easy. Some days, I miss it, and it makes me sad. During these times, my mind drifts off, and I think what my career could have been if I had not made the changes I did.

I'm fortunate that I am visited by these thoughts less frequently as time passes. However, I know the decision to work my way off the road was a good one. This decision has been validated in many different—dare I say—spiritual ways.

Tuesday, September 15th—7:00 P.M.

You know, I knew it was too good to be true. Three flights down and only one to go, and that one got me. As I deplaned from my Chicago flight, I was greeted with that word I hate so much: Washington Dulles, "Delayed."

I tried to jump on a National flight, but I was wait-listed. Now that I don't fly as much, I don't exactly go to the top. Ten minutes before the flight was to take off, they finished calling the wait list. I went up to see how close I had gotten and found out that I was still 25 people away. Part of me felt a nostalgic memory of having the miles of the past to jump to the top. Another part of me pitied those who did rise to the top . . .

I am not what most would call a religious person, but I believe we have a purpose, and I believe we are given signs. Some of these signs are small, like not rising to the top of a waiting list. Others are a lot more dramatic. I can't even count the number of colleagues I've come across who haven fallen, and by fallen, I mean totally dysfunctional lives, marriages, and families. The simple words of the Reverend Jim Casey in John Steinbeck's *Grapes of Wrath* provide meaningful commentary on this matter:

> *There ain't no sin and there ain't no virtue. There's just stuff people do. It's all part of the same thing. And some of the things folks do is nice and some ain't nice, but that's as far as any man got a right to say.*

This particular chapter took me longer to write than the rest of the entire book. The addiction to travel that seizes so many Road Warriors haunts me to this day, and most likely it always will. I do not want to appear as a hypocrite or traitor to my fellow Road Warriors. I am simply a man who needed to speak out and share what I have seen and felt from these many years on the road.

When I was in college, I rode a motorcycle for a short period. My uncle once saw me riding and gave me this pearl of wisdom. He said, "There's only two types of motorcycle riders—them that's been down, and them that's going down!"

When I see Road Warriors who have become slaves to their jobs and have put their personal lives at risk doing it, I see these types of people falling into one of two categories: "Them that's been down, and them that's going down."

What is your exit strategy? The final question you need to ask yourself is a difficult one. It's difficult, because it requires thought relating to failure. If we don't have a plan to celebrate success, we can sure think of one in a hurry. What plan do we implement if we do not succeed? When will that plan be implemented? What's the definition we intend to use for failure? As I said, these are difficult questions.

They are so difficult, for many years I regarded even the thought of some of those questions as a sign of weakness. Once, before a big race I was competing in, I was interviewed by the *Washington Post.* I eagerly answered every question—that was until the reporter hit me with his version of an exit strategy question.

He asked me, "What will you do if you do not complete this triathlon?"

I was puzzled by the question, and stalling, asked him to repeat it. I had honestly never let that thought cross my mind. After he repeated the question, I not only told him I had never thought about it, I told him I would *never* let my mind think about it. To me, it was a sign of weakness to even consider failure. I told him I would not answer that question, and after a little prodding from his end, we moved on.

> **Friday, July 21st—10:00 P.M.**
> What a strange paradox I find myself locked into. The more I travel, the more money I make. The more money I make, the more we are able to do as a family. Sounds good, but it isn't working.
>
> The more I travel, the angrier my wife and kids become. Once upon a time, they all wanted me to work hard, earn a lot of money, and provide nicely for them. Now, I'm no longer a warrior, I'm a villain. The rewards of my travels no longer seem to please anyone.

This paradox seems to mirror what history now calls the "Vietnam Syndrome." At first it seemed to be a just war, and had some measure of political support. As the war intensified, that political support eroded away. Our goals became as unclear as our ultimate intentions. Finally, forced to abandon the battlefield, and then having been ridiculed and humiliated upon their return to America, the generation of military leaders who rose to the highest ranks of the armed forces in the late seventies and eighties determined never again to risk American lives in combat unless they were certain of a strong domestic consensus.

The Vietnam War taught us many lessons, perhaps the most important being the need for a strong consensus, and the need for an exit strategy. Years later, General Colin Powell actually introduced us to this term as we prepared for the Gulf War. Years later we were introduced to this term again in the Iraqi war.

An exit strategy is not a sign of weakness, as I mistakenly thought years ago. It's a sign of strength and intelligence. Planning an exit strategy is not planning for failure. It is simply planning and preparing for any and all options. As I've stated a number of times, to survive as a Road Warrior, you must have the support of your family. Additionally, you must have a plan in place to remove yourself from the road eventually: that is, an exit strategy.

The last of the twelve steps of personal recovery says, "Having had a spiritual awakening as the result of these steps, we tried to carry this message to addicted personalities and to practice these principles in all our affairs." I hope the words in this chapter are of comfort to the struggling Road Warrior, or even to the struggling Road Warrior's loved ones. Approach this situation as you would any addiction. My hopes are that I have fulfilled the twelfth step of this process by carrying my message to you.

CHAPTER THIRTEEN

The End of My Confessions

Thursday, July 7th—9:30 P.M.

This is a rarity. I'm sitting in front of my dear friend and travel companion—my laptop—and I just don't have much to say. It's been a long, long trip and I have one more night in this cold and impersonal hotel room.

Work has gone well, flights were on time, the weather is good, as was my meal tonight. Anything and everything that could have gone well on this trip did, and in spite of it all, I can't wait to go home and be with my family. It's not utopia, and it's not perfect, but it's my home, my wife, and my kids. Despite our imperfections, we are a family and anything here pales by comparison.

I guess I had something to say tonight after all. To borrow a line from The Wizard of Oz, *"There's no place like home."*

I suppose I always will be a Road Warrior. I have spent nearly twenty years of my life conducting business on the road, and if I am so blessed, I might just spend another twenty years on the road. When I started this book, I said, "My real occupation is to survive and thrive on the road." Now I realize that isn't completely true. My real occupation is to survive on the road so I can thrive at home.

You see, as this book comes to an end, I have one final admission. Being a Road Warrior may be exciting, rewarding, and an exhilarating way of life, but it doesn't come close to being where we are all needed the most—at home. Home is where all real Road Warriors belong. Home, to the most important people in our lives—more important than any client we'll ever work for, any meeting we'll ever attend. Home, to the simple pleasures that await us all. Home, to the sheer delight of being greeted with a hug, a story, or a smile.

I'm proud of the books I have written, but I truly hope that the message in this book rings loud and clear. Perhaps you too can take advantage of the time you spend on the road learning from your many adventures. More important, though, maybe you can begin to strategize how to manage your time on the road without sacrificing your family or friends.

When you use your travel wisely, you can become a wiser person. If you must travel, travel intelligently. Stop and process what's around you. You don't have to be a Road Warrior to observe your surroundings. The question is, what will you do with the information that's around you?

I hope you take my advice and keep a journal. Keep your eyes open, watch more carefully, write it down, capture it, and actively study it. You just never know when someone will cross your path and teach you a lesson, provide you with a reminder, or maybe just make you laugh . . .

Thursday, October 19th–8:00 P.M.

What a character that was. I just got up to my hotel room, but I had to break out the laptop for this one. I just got out of a cab, and handed my cab driver a real nice tip. Heck, he earned it. I came out of the airport, jumped in his cab, and right away the chatter started.

"How you doing tonight?" he asked. I just wasn't in the mood and grunted a "fine" back at him.

"Hot enough for you here?" he spat out.

"Sure." Not tonight, pal, I just want to get to my hotel. It had been a long day—couldn't he figure it out yet? I just didn't want to talk.

He simply wasn't giving up. "Where you from?" came next.

"Oh, please, would you just give it up?" I thought. I gave him another grunted response: "Washington, D.C."

With that, he opened up his glove compartment and rummaged around for a minute or two. Finally, he produced a little Redskin helmet on a string. He then hung it from his rearview mirror and gave me a big smile. According to my cabbie friend, he was "a huge Redskin fan!"

Now, who knows how many helmets he had in that glove compartment, and who knows how often he pulled this little scam, but he had done his homework. He knew just enough names to sound credible. He also opened me up for conversation like a pro.

Yep, I bit. By the time we got to the hotel, my meter read $25. I gave him $40 and he didn't even flinch. As a matter of fact, he looked like he was quite used to getting tipped well. As for me, I felt he earned it. To begin with, he pulled me out of my travel funk and delivered me to the hotel in a really good mood. Besides, it took guts for a Dallas cabdriver to hang a Redskin helmet in his car and drive through town!

Road Warriors aren't the only people who think quickly and maximize their opportunities. At the risk of becoming overly spiritual, in my mind, these people are there for a reason. They are there to teach us, and give us an opportunity to gain wisdom. We have a choice. We can blindly walk by, haphazardly allow the more persistent of the messengers to reach us occasionally, or truly use each and every opportunity that is before us to learn.

And now my story is told. What started for me as a means to an end became my greatest teacher. What I've tried to share with you, my reader, came as a result of the most important business tool I have ever acquired—my personal thoughts. I would not have been capable of learning the lessons I have attempted to share with you without my journal. This business tool has been my greatest Road Warrior companion, coach and tutor. I cannot implore you enough to use this tool and learn from your own life as well.

I once read a story that puts this all in perspective. A reporter asked a farmer to divulge the secret behind his corn, which won the state fair contest year after year. The farmer confessed it was all because he shared his seed corn with his neighbors. "Why do you share your best seed corn with your neighbors when they're entering the same contest each year as well?" asked the reporter. "Why," said the farmer, "didn't you know? The wind picks up pollen from the ripening corn and swirls it from field to field. If my neighbors grew inferior corn, cross-pollination would steadily degrade the quality of my corn. If I am to grow good corn, I must help my neighbor do the same."

So it is with other situations in our lives. I believe that those who want to be successful must help their neighbors be successful. Those who gain wisdom by their mistakes must help others live better lives by teaching what they have learned, for the value of a life is measured by the lives it touches. And those who choose to be happy must help others find happiness, for the welfare of each is bound up with the welfare of all.

We work to survive and we survive to acquire wisdom. Road Warriors, if you remember nothing from the words I have written, remember this: Nothing will ever take the place of the times you spend with the people you care about and those who care about you. When work, travel, and family all come together, sometimes the simplest messages can say the most.

A prized possession from my daughter Jessie:

I hope I've been able to act as a tour guide, one of the many that in a sense you've probably walked by. There's just so much more to what is in front of us every day. If I've opened your eyes to look a little deeper, articulate what you are seeing, and learn from these lessons, then the journey has been worthwhile. Thanks for listening.

Now I have a favor to ask of you. The greatest joy I receive from my writing is hearing from you, my reader. If you are up to it, I would like to hear from you. Perhaps a story or lesson touched you in a certain way, or maybe you would like to share one of your favorite Road Warrior stories. In any case, I've created a Web site with you in mind, and would love for you to drop by. For stories, blogs, travel tips, resources, and more, please go to www.Wayoftheroadwarrior.com.

Also, feel free to drop me a line at:
E-mail . . .
     RoadWarrior@Jolles.com
Write . . .
     Rob Jolles
     P.O. Box 930
     Great Falls, VA 22066
For information on the seminars I conduct, visit . . .
     www.Jolles.com

ACKNOWLEDGMENTS

My children, Danny, Jessie, and Sandy, who have endured my many nights on the road, shared a few with me themselves, and have never wavered in their encouragement of the job I was bred to perform.

Sam Quaye, my cab driver, who has been a part of almost every journey I have taken, and become a steady and enduring friend for many years.

Bill Sanzenbacher, one of my many captains, only this captain touched me with his steady tones of compassion. We're always listening.

Mary Wright, whose skillful editing, remarkable literary wisdom, and stunning ability to preserve the spirit of my message leaves me more grateful than she will ever know.

Neal Maillet, my editor at Jossey-Bass. Without your belief in my message there would be no book. Without your feedback, encouragement, and editorial suggestions, there would be no polish. I consider it a privilege to call you my friend.

My parents, Lee and Judy Jolles, whose optimistic perspective on life instilled within me a similar trait. In retrospect, what could be more important for any Road Warrior whose existence is littered with challenges than an obscene level of positive thinking.

And finally, my wife, Ronni, who literally saved my life by teaching me the most critical lesson a partner could teach. She taught me that home is where I belong, and that working toward that end is the noblest of acts that a Road Warrior can perform.

THE AUTHOR

Rob Jolles—a best-selling author and professional speaker—knows the life of a Road Warrior firsthand from twenty-two years' experience and more than two million miles in the air alone. He is no casual observer to a profession that requires consistent travel. With his trusty black roll-on garment bag and black laptop case, he is a participating member of the emerging culture of Road Warriors.

He is also president of Jolles Associates, Inc., an independent training consulting firm with a client list that reads like a Who's Who of Fortune 500 companies, including Toyota, Disney, NASA, Nortel, a dozen universities, and more than fifty financial institutions. He is represented by over a dozen speakers bureaus and conducts seminars all over the world. He lives in Great Falls, Virginia.